The Last Disciple

The Last Disciple

*A Contemporary Primer on the Theology and Practice
of the American Pentecostal Movement*

DAVID PAFFORD

WIPF & STOCK · Eugene, Oregon

THE LAST DISCIPLE
A Contemporary Primer on the Theology and Practice of the American Pentecostal Movement

Copyright © 2011 David Pafford. All rights reserved. Except for brief quotations in critical publications or reviews, no part of this book may be reproduced in any manner without prior written permission from the publisher. Write: Permissions, Wipf and Stock Publishers, 199 W. 8th Ave., Suite 3, Eugene, OR 97401.

Wipf & Stock
An Imprint of Wipf and Stock Publishers
199 W. 8th Ave., Suite 3
Eugene, OR 97401
www.wipfandstock.com

ISBN 13: 978-1-61097-621-3

Manufactured in the U.S.A.

All scripture quotations, unless otherwise indicated, are taken from the Holy Bible, New International Version®, NIV®. Copyright ©1973, 1978, 1984 by Biblica, Inc.™ Used by permission of Zondervan. All rights reserved worldwide.

To Elizabeth, whatever we lose will be our gain; we count it inexpressibly tied to our debt of love.

To parents whose love for the church is best expressed in their integrity and solidarity throughout every season of life.

Contents

Preface ix
Acknowledgments xi
Introduction xiii

PART 1 ECCLESIOLOGY: A LOOK AT THE CHURCH 1

1. The First Churches 3
2. Identity 10
3. Pastoral Theology in Motion 28
4. Challenges 55
5. Best Practices 88

PART 2 CHRISTOLOGY: THINKING LIKE JESUS ABOUT THE CHURCH 99

6. The Incarnational Nature of God 101
7. The Image of God 107
8. Being Born in Christ 120
9. The Kingdom of God 124
10. The Role of Isaiah in the Life of Jesus 135
11. Jesus' Eschatology and the Call to Faithfulness 148
12. Conclusion 154

Glossary of Terms 157
Bibliography 161

Preface

This book is about the discovery, practice, and hermeneutics of the local church. It comes out of my love for church, which itself comes from my being loved by the people of the church. The roots of many believers run deep under several denominations and traditions. My roots twist and turn through a variety of church traditions, some fertile and full of nutrients, still others hard with piteous polity that have produced stability. Nonetheless, my roots have drunk deeply from the waters of Pentecostalism. I'm a third-generation Pentecostal, which, as you may know, is rather rare. This informs my view of the church, its mission, and its presence.

Readers from Pentecostal and Charismatic backgrounds can and should apply this work to a variety of ecclesiological studies. Readers from these backgrounds will find that this work is unlike other books from these traditions. That is, this is not a major theological work on Spirit Baptism or some of the other charismata. Simply speaking, so many works have done an excellent job of introducing and discussing these issues at length.

Clark Pinnock says that if God the Father is seen through the Son, and the Son through the Spirit, then perhaps the Spirit is seen through the saints of the church. We want to know how the Spirit is seen through the church and its saints. The question, then, is who are these people of God? In the Pentecostal tradition, they are a pilgrim people, a people on the move, in relation to the mission of the church. Thus, this church is a group of churches constantly on the move. A Spirit-led church such as this is not simply one on the move, but one headed toward a stronger christological witness; and the result of its reliance on the Spirit makes it more Christlike.

Preface

Indeed, the church is a Spirit-created, Spirit-breathed, and Spirit-sustained phenomenon. Still, the church is human: anthropological in its nature and sociological in its influence. Near the end of chapter 2 of Ephesians, Paul says that the church is housed in human flesh. This is to say that the church is neither sterile nor static. Frankly, "doing church" is a messy business, especially in a modern church where the hierarchy is decentralized and spiritual gifts are dispensed as they are needed. Anything can happen. People come in from the cold in real need, with real baggage, and those of us already inside are asked to clean up. It's messy, but it's also beautiful, with elements of the sublime peeking around the corner now and then. At certain moments—if you're tuned into it— you will see the natural outer layers peel back like Christmas paper to reveal another, otherwise hidden, reality. In this way we see the Spirit within. Most of us tend to decorate and doctor the exteriors of things. Unfortunately, this preoccupation with the exterior is like receiving a gift and admiring the paper in which it's wrapped, rather than unwrapping the gift to see the true treasure inside. The true treasure of the church is the Spirit. And Jesus reminds us to simply not beautify the exterior, but to participate with the divine through the Spirit.

If indeed the Spirit is seen through the saints of the church, then we must study the church, which is always on the move. Thus, we must attempt to define who we are and who we are becoming. And if it is the Spirit that ultimately defines the church, then ultimately we are simply looking for where the Spirit is peeking out.

Let's unwrap the gift.

Acknowledgments

T HE LAST Disciple is a product of a bunch of folks who deserve thanks.

First is the district team in Columbia. Thanks to the Brewers and the Hunts for putting up with my intensity for this project and the one coming next. I'd like to give special thanks to Dr. Ray Brewer who is a true friend to the church. I'd like to thank many of the pastors and leaders in Missouri to whom I have bounced off ideas, or have simply done life with. We, more than anyone, know that the doing of church can at times be a grand experiment.

I also want to thank the many friends of North Central University, Fuller Theological Seminary, and William Woods University, including the hundreds of friends both past and present, namely Ryan Decker, Matt Brown, Dave Savage, Aaron Bannin, Chris Mancl, Paul Hurckman, Aaron Smith, and countless others. Thanks to team FivestAr from WWU, Amy, Kerri, Jeremy, and Brian who put up with me while we collectively finished our MBAs.

I want to thank Glen Menzies and Gordon Anderson for their commitment to both the church and the academy. I'd like to thank Phil Hilliard and Cecil Robeck for several conversations we had at Bethany Church during my time at Fuller. Thanks to Amy Anderson for helping me discover, or rediscover, resources and giving tips along the way.

I spent a lot of time writing at our campgrounds, on the road, and at home. I could not have done that without the kind of support I get on a regular basis from my wife. A work like this one included many nights where I got dinner and then went to the office to work. It also included talking through theological concepts with her, af-

Acknowledgments

ter she did research for the University all day. Thanks babe, I am blessed. Finally, thanks to our parents who want the church to be the church in all ways.

Introduction

THERE IS a question that has been rolling around in my head for weeks: Who will be the last disciple? Certainly, there must be a final person on earth who will be Christ's last disciple. Perhaps a better question is this: Will this last disciple exist because the return of Christ was imminent upon their conversion, or will this person be the last disciple because he or she failed to translate the practices of Jesus to the next person? After all, this is a *real battle* with casualties on both sides, good and evil. Imagine if a church could look into the future and see the last disciple it would produce. Would it have an impact?

This is similar to knowing the exact day and time you will die. If we were to know the final moment of our existence, would it change how we live? I'm willing to bet that, likewise, this foreknowledge would change how this last disciple would walk in the Christian faith. Would this person, armed with such knowledge, strive all the harder to convert nonbelievers into authentic followers of Jesus Christ? I would like to think so.

The Last Disciple is a book for people who care enough about *doing church* that they want to evaluate *why they do it*. The first portion of this book provides a solid theological basis for what the church is doing. It is designed to help readers better understand key aspects of the church and the thinking that created them by discussing the modern church's identity, its theology, the challenges that it faces, and its best practices as it attempts to make disciples. This work not only provides a theological scope of the present but also sets a theological nexus for the future.

The second portion of *The Last Disciple* is about Christ and his relationship to ministry in the church. Here we look at exactly

Introduction

who Christ is, and how his communication is a vital part of the life of the believer and the church. Finally, this book investigates the connections between Christ and the church through a discussion of Jesus' favorite topic: the kingdom of God.

Part 1

Ecclesiology:
A Look at the Church

THE CHURCH has a mixed history of introspection, and I would submit that a church with a strong sense of identity is better equipped to fulfill its purpose. It is my hope that this book will give your faith community a better sense of how to discover its identity. In the next several chapters we are going to discover, and in some cases rediscover, what makes a local church a church.

A local community must do more than form its concept of the gospel around the local church. Indeed, the implications of personal narratives, architecture, a church's history, technology uses, philosophy, and even church governance structures are huge factors in the formation of a local community interpretation. It is so critical to understand how each of these is charged theologically.

The formation of good ministry practices comes from a solid theological foundation. However, it appears that local churches have lost their way in terms of service, and in so doing have inadvertently created a theological void. It is therefore vital that local churches reinvest in developing good theological models. This subject is investigated here.

Today's churches must also rise to meet many other challenges including urbanization, discipleship, postmodernity, developing relational ministries, eliminating cultural irrelevance, and

THE LAST DISCIPLE

addressing issues of self-centeredness. A basic understanding of these challenges will help a local church to meet the real-world needs of its community. Finally, this part studies some best practices that a local church can employ to meet the needs of its community. These practices include good communication, developing a biblical social justice mindset, and creating dependable communities that can trust one another through embodied selflessness, truth, and intercession.

1

The First Churches

What then shall we say? When you come together, everyone has a hymn, or a word of instruction, a revelation, a tongue or an interpretation. All of these must be done for the strengthening of the church.

1 CORINTHIANS 14:26 (NIV)

IMAGINE WHAT this passage from 1 Corinthians would have sounded like to its original readers. Probably, it would have been read aloud to them. Maybe over a red, crackling fire, a small gathering of believers would meet near the back of a dark, cold alley to listen to it. Imagine how a passerby might have viewed this tattered group, gathered as they were on humble fringes of the great city of Corinth. This passerby might have wondered why they uttered such odd things in such a profane place. "After all," he might mumble, "such things as prophesy, hymns, and revelations belong in the pantheon of gods, or at the Temple of Apollo."

However, like the prostitutes at the Temple of Apollo, Corinth is a city of façade. It is a veneer of beautiful skyscrapers. Temples of worship and civic structures push through the clouds, but underneath them is an ugly underbelly. For this cold alley is part of the new Corinth, reborn from old. The buildings in this part of town are no more than one hundred years old. They were rebuilt after Julius Caesar began reconstruction in 44 BC.[1] Here, the city is populated with artisans and slaves, most who have come from

---

1. Fee, *Corinthians*, 1.

THE LAST DISCIPLE

Rome. And because new money attracts people like a dead carcass attracts flies, there are thousands of people flooding into the city. This ragged congregation mirrors the population of its city. Jews, Greeks, Barbarians, slaves, and freemen are gathered here. These people are what some civil leaders have called human waste.

The passerby slows when he hears someone from the group suddenly break forth in song. "How bizarre!" the man thinks aloud. "What type of religious group is this? No special building, no specific order of service, or even a specialized priest or leader." What makes it odder, still, is that this hodgepodge band keeps croaking peculiarly about one God. "Atheists! Not only are they so myopic to think only one god exists, but they don't even go to a particular temple to worship it."

Someone from the group notes the man's gaze and invites him in. By now, his curiosity is piqued, and he can't resist. He enters the circle.

The singer continues his song. He is a fellow Greek, of all things. And his song is one of encouragement. "We are hard pressed on every side," he sings, "but in him we'll find rest despite the rising tide. We are perplexed, but not in despair though we are fined unfair. Persecuted by man but not abandoned by his hand. Struck down, but nonetheless amen."

The beauty of the tune is overwhelming, and the passerby remarks to himself how lucidly the lyrics draw the picture of this group, surrounded as they are by hard-pressed clay on every side, but nonetheless finding solidarity in their God.

As the man's curiosity wanes, he notes the mutual encouragement among the members of this group. He sees the value and feels the strengthening of this group as they build up one another. He thinks to himself: *What a curious gathering! What a funny calling . . . ek-kalo . . . ekklesia!* The man finds this little word game humorous. Nonetheless, he is amazed by the group. Frankly, he's awestruck. But he has appointments to keep, and so, despite his amazement, he departs the group and continues on his way.

What this man experienced on the "mean" streets of Corinth was what some would characterize as a church. Key facets and elements allow this gathering of people to be part of the institution God created, not only as a representative of things visible, and invisible, to come but also as a phenomenon called the *kingdom of God*. He called it an "ekklesia." When we study it, we call it *ecclesiology*.

ECCLESIOLOGY

Classically put, ecclesiology is the study of what is necessary for an institution to be a church—an ecclesia. Over the centuries, theologians have asked the constitutional question of necessitation: What makes a local church part of *the* church? For the Catholics, ecclesial constitution requires a priest and a mass because these are the methods through which grace is dispensed. For the Reformers, the requirements of necessitation are the Word and the Sacraments; Luther and Calvin would argue that an institution without these elements simply does not constitute a church.

The Roots of Pentecostalism

Pentecostalism is a modern movement that began at the turn of the twentieth century. Founded in an era of rapid social changes and notable attitudinal shifts, the Pentecostal Church has always been challenged to reflect on and express its self-understanding in a fashion that is faithful to the tradition of the Pentecostal movement. As I research and reflect, I marvel at the changes this church has experienced during the past one hundred years. It is true that, in its growth, the Pentecostal movement stands second only to the Catholic Church. Pentecostalism, as large as it is, can remain relevant by carefully receiving insight from the ingenuity and strategy of some of the secular disciplines.

Within the last fifty years, we have seen the Pentecostal Church move into mainstream religious mass production. This has had unfortunate results in terms of institutional values, which include a highly volatile prosperity gospel. This breed of Pentecostalism has strayed far from the Pentecostalism of the early twentieth century. Conversely, some of the aging structures have also become Pentecostal in name only. The result is a fragmented church model. These competing models are, at times, at odds with each other insofar as denominations must reconcile their traditions with an ever-changing, ever-expanding worldwide community. It is an issue that demands attention and reflection. The ability of traditional, contemporary, and unique church models to be critical of their own preferences is essential.

What transcends denominational history is the important theological axiom that all Pentecostals rely on the Spirit of God. This is the same Spirit that breathes life into the church and moves it toward the eschaton.

Pentecostal Ecclesiology

The subject of Pentecostal ecclesiology has received little, if any, explicit articulation. Perhaps, in our Free Church approach where each local church is sovereign, we find this esoteric practice to be a waste of time. After all, we are evangelistically pressed toward the eschaton. Our pragmatic approach has thus left questions of precision for those more interested figuring out *what a church is*, rather than having church itself. And so, our stance has been to leave those questions for theological skirmishes: Our business is the spread of the mission of the church, the missio dei. Indeed, it is the mission that defines us.

Perhaps, in the end, Pentecostalism's greatest legacy will be indigenous principles of grassroots movements in developing countries. It is a remarkable feat to create contextualization models that pull people of a given ethnic group toward the gospel without synchronization. As a result, today, Pentecostalism is the largest-growing segment of the church in the world. We've gone

The First Churches

from zero to four hundred million in less than a hundred years.[2] There's nothing new about this information. Nonetheless, much of the established movement of Pentecostalism in the United States is denominationalizing and, in the wake of one of the greatest evangelistic spreads of the gospel, the church that remains begs the question of what constitutes a Pentecostal Church.

Pentecostalism and Charismatic movements share some commonality, but there are also differences. As is pointed out by Kärkkäinen, "Pentecostalism represents a revival movement with a restorationist tendency and consequently a low view of history and tradition."[3] While not true of all Charismatic groups, many Charismatics at least share the history of their tradition. For example, Catholic Charismatic groups emphasis that the gifts have always been part of the church in one way or another. The Pentecostalism and Charismatic movements also find points of distinction in the dates of their respective foundings—classical Pentecostalism begins in 1906 and Charismatic movements begin in the 1960s.[4] While these dates represent important points of history, a focus on minutia of divergence between peoples of like-faith detracts from the mission of the church itself. As such, I will not go to great lengths to find divergences within the Pentecostal Church, and will do so only in an effort to describe the complexity of this ever-growing movement.

Definition

Pentecostal ecclesiology, by any stretch, is missional. The mantra of missional ecclesiology is that, without a mission, a church is not a church. In Pentecostal circles, when you say church, you're saying mission. Even so, we've lost some of the connections to our theological body in regard to mission. We have lost our sense of

2. Hollenweger, "Historical Roots," 3.
3. Kärkkäinen, *Introduction to Ecclesiology*, 76.
4. Burgess, *New International Dictionary*, xxii.

being. And without a theological depth of *being*, we will lose the rational for *doing* mission. Without doubt, many Pentecostals understand the value of continuing our mission as we await Christ's return, and we will continue the mission until that great day. But, we may not have a strong connection to the theological framework of the movement itself. Just like in the body, ligaments can grow weak when they are not stretched. The ligaments are what cause the body to maintain its skeletal structure. We are having trouble defining *being*. The ligaments are dissolving. We've lost the idea of the church as *being*. The concept of the church as a mystical body, where you sort of just "be there," [5] is a lost idea to the modern Pentecostal.

Indeed, true believers are the church embodied. Embodiment elicits this idea of a metaphysical wholeness. Wholeness means that believers are the visible church in the truest sense of its physicality and spirituality. To quote Miller, "You do not have a soul. You are a soul. You have a body."[6] This notion helps us not just to think of the church as some romantic ideal, but rather as the realistic hope of the world. Nonetheless, when people in a given church explore questions of ecclesiology (whether they truly understand the gravity of their question), they often include "mission" as part of the study, both in the word and in the activity of the church. This framing convention, more often than not, is a window that simply allows people to identify themselves in terms of *what we do*, but not *who we are* . . . And all too often, questions of ecclesiology end with answers of mere identification. We, as Pentecostals know *what we do*. But, *who are we* Pentecostals a century later? Are we just another mission movement turned denomination? Many fear this to be the case. It is a discovery that has caused a surprising reaction.

Who are we? Are we Pentecostals who have lost touch with our theological *being*, consigned to drawing denominational distinctions among competing factions? Is this the legacy of the char-

---

5. Ott, *Fundamentals of Catholic Dogma*, 312.
6. Miller, *Canticle for Leibowitz*, 295.

ismatic blowing of the Spirit in the last fifty years? And if we are left wondering *who we are*, we will only ask how we are different? Distinction seems to be a sordid approach for our world; and identification is not found in the attempt to define *what we are not*.

Again, *who are we*? Forgive my insistence and my small independent streak, but I am trying to look at Pentecostal ecclesiology through the eyes of today's culture. It is a lucid perspective that helps us see how others see our churches. This is an exercise that gives us insight.

In the Sermon on the Mount, Jesus talks about how we perceive the reality of what we think of our neighbors. His prescription for avoiding grandiose self-deception is to first assess our own failures: to see ourselves for ourselves. Jesus teaches us only that after we understand ourselves can we work on helping our neighbors fix the reality of what they think of us.

Thus, who we are as individuals is informed by how others see us. In the same way, our church is defined by how it is perceived from without. And it is my hope that along our journey we see ourselves through new eyes. In so doing we will be open to criticism and critique, but, ultimately, we will be open to understanding: why people are looking elsewhere for spirituality. Let us find meaning beyond façade. Let us not take refuge only in grand cathedrals that scrape the sky. Indeed, let us take inspiration from slaves gathered around poor fires in back alleys. Let us understand how both the mighty and the downtrodden see us, so that we can win them in the name of Christ. This is our great mission. This is who we are.

2

Identity

IDENTITY IS theological. If the word is being replaced by image then people, consciously or unconsciously, are deriving more theological identity from the church they walk into than could be put into a book. This, of course, presumes they actually walk into a church. Theology—and, more importantly, theological interpretation—is more often a product of personal experience than it is from words we read on a page or hear from a pulpit. The implication is that the architecture, customary worship actions, pew placement, and visibility of a church have more effect on theological identity than the actual message. What the local church looks like, what it acts upon, how old the building is, how old its members are, what issues it stresses or does not stress—that is the gospel according to a particular community because these are what that community directly experience. This is sometimes called a hermeneutic. Cultural hermeneutics play a huge role in the interpretation of events and the perceptions of reality. The local church, not the Bible, is the lens through which a given community interprets the gospel.

ELEMENTS THAT SHAPE THEOLOGICAL INTERPRETATION

If the local church is the hermeneutic of the gospel to its community, you can imagine how differently the gospel can be interpreted by this same community. This raises yet more questions. In what ways did the founders of a church consider the community

Identity

when they established their church in the manner they did? Some churches maintain a view of historical preservation in their approach, while others seem to focus almost entirely on what is new. Churches are in converted warehouses, stadiums, schools, homes, and bars. They are on TV, streamed over the Internet, and tweeted. Some churches are laser-focused on one type of person or demographic, such as the cowboy, the young man, or the family. What are all of these creators and leaders saying to their community?

As far as the larger community is concerned, this interpretation is the church's identity. This interpretation may be an accurate portrayal of the church's mission. It may not be accurate. Thus, it is incumbent upon the church to translate its true persona to its community. In this regard, perception is reality. The church must maintain its role as a meaningful contributor to its larger community. Members of that church must seriously consider how their church is perceived from without. Perception equals action, and members express the mission of their church through their involvement in the community. Indeed, a church shapes its perception in the very manner that it practices its mission. It almost goes without saying that church members must believe the church persona, especially because believing in it reinforces the continuation of the church's interpretation to its community.

Praying for the Children

Then little children were brought to Jesus for him to place his hands on them and pray for them. But the disciples rebuked those who brought them. Jesus said, "Let the little children come to me, and stop hindering them[1]*, for the kingdom of heaven belongs to such as these."*

MATTHEW 19:13–14 (NIV)

---

1. Author's emphasis based on the Greek text—(imperative tense).

Prayer is theological. I was made consciously aware of how even small details are theologically charged. I was living in Los Angeles, serving on staff at a multi-ethnic church in one of the northern suburbs. During our Sunday morning services, one of the pastors would give a prayer of dismissal from the pulpit for the children, and then we would dismiss our children from the sanctuary so they could go to children's church. They would all run toward the exit on the far left side of the sanctuary, wait for the pastor to finish the prayer, and then run out the exit. Without intention, our children looked as though they were being cast aside every service, and the pastoral prayer added insult to that injury. This prayer, as it happened, often remarked that children were the future of the church. Thus, our church actually repelled families with a practice that was meant to attract them. Some sitting in the service, seeing how the children were on the far left side and the pastor was behind the pulpit, subconsciously perceived a level of irony to what was happening.

One day, the pastoral staff began discussing changing how we dismissed children. We invited the children to the stage before our prayer, and then had our staff come off the stage to pray with them. By physically centering our children in the sanctuary, we theologically reinforced to our congregation the value we placed on the children of our families. Please understand that this small detail had little correlation to how we actually treated our children in that church. Our church had a long way to go toward improving our children's ministries. Nonetheless, this example illustrates how even moving a group of kids during a service provides a theologically powerful statement about what a church values. *How we pray* is theological.

Here's the problem with my little antidote: it's not an isolated incident. This is happening all over the country, time and time again. As unintended as these theological images are, cumulatively, they have become a constant value statement that youth must overcome when they pass through the doors of our churches.

Identity

Moreover, youths do not have the sociological sophistication to explain to our churches that these theological narratives, happening every Sunday, are powerful images.

Images and narratives such as these are valued much higher by our youths than are sermons that can be rehearsed and practiced. Thus, the picture being illustrated to many of our youths is that the church is either an unjust organization or an organization that simply doesn't understand them.

Architecture and Experience

Architecture is theological. A church located in the downtown area of a mid-Missouri city constructed an addition to their church. The addition included a building to house the church's education center. The church is surrounded by a variety of businesses in this downtown location. North of the church is another church, a theater, and some restaurants. West of the church are more restaurants. Finally, to the church's south is a popular university bar that sits rather close to the church. This new addition featured windows on every side except one: the one that faced the bar. This side had no windows. All of the other walls featured large windowpanes that allowed in outside light, illuminating the interior of the education wing.

Now, to a person knowledgeable about the appropriate set-up of classrooms, the absence of windows makes quite a bit of sense: a solid back wall is an asset from an educator's point of view. I noticed that all the classrooms were designed such that the teacher would stand on the side of the classroom with the solid wall. This design allows students to focus on the instructor without distraction, yet allows students to enjoy some direct natural light. This design also allows those on the outside to see into the classrooms as if they, too, were students. This is no coincidence. In this respect, it is a good design. However, one of my wife's non-church-going friends commented on the windowless aspect of the church's architecture.

THE LAST DISCIPLE

She said, "It looks as though they just want to cloister themselves away."

Now if the local church is the hermeneutic through which this community interprets the gospel, then what the above comment represents is a theological statement of exclusion, rather than of invitation.

Historical Experience

History informs our theological hermeneutic. Understanding the experience of our people requires that we think about their history. Historical events can alter the theological lens through which we interpret our world, just as it can alter the lens through which our forefathers viewed theirs.

Prior to World War I, two major theological schools emphasized their eschatological confessions. Many of the theologically liberal mainline Christian denominations underscored their postmillennial eschatological view with the merit of progress. They were not without many evidences to corroborate their position. The enlightenment produced incredible advances in science and technology, and with them came advances in the humanities. One can trace our theological schools of thought back to Kant, Descartes, and a host of thinkers from the enlightenment period that eventually manifested in the theology of the late nineteenth century. Even as the world continued to improve, many Christians nonetheless seemed to think that they were going to hand the keys of the kingdom to Christ. However, the Fundamentalists and their contemporaries highlighted the biblical warning against the hubris of humanity, and emphasized the continual deterioration of humanity. Many considered the Fundamentalist theological affirmation to be an ad hoc flaw with little, biblically, to substantiate their claim. After all, with this theological affirmation came many extra-biblical prophetic claims about eschatological details that were not only absurd, but also misleading.

Identity

As a result, during the early twentieth century more Christians believed in the construct of human progress (postmillennial) than in the descent of humanity (premillennial). They were looking at Scripture with a pre–World War I hermeneutic. While this period of time produced many valuable advances, it also produced incredible hubris. Then World Wars I and II took place, and humanity again realized the depths of its depravity. Even with some of their eschatological absurdity, the Fundamentalists' theological claims were considered by Christians (in general, and over time) to have more validity with regard to a theology of human regression. So, these historical events substantiated the theological claim of human regression present in premillennialism. Today, premillennialism is a more accepted school of thought in the evangelical world. Our history informed our hermeneutic.

EMERGING TRENDS

History is currently informing the interpretation of human etiology, salvation, and the role of the church in the kingdom of God. We can, of course, only provide a degree of conjecture, given the closeness of the object in view. Nonetheless, close study reveals some emerging trends that are more recent in their development but affect the hermeneutic of a church both from within its own walls and within the community.

Oversimplified Approach to Scripture

The first emerging trend is the oversimplified approaches our churches take toward Scripture. This is a cultural shift from both within and from outside the church. Even some nonbelievers are surprised by the laissez-faire attitude with which we, as believers, wield Scripture. In our general studies and interpretations, we take very little time to investigate the implications of our claims. We take what works and dismiss the difficult questions that our interpretations reveal. This is typified in the practice of engraving our name on our Bible. We don't even think twice about it. We want to stake our claim on truth, but we don't want to live with the personal implications truth claims on us. I believe this refusal, in itself, betrays perhaps something more sinister: that we, as a community of believers, have stopped taking the Scriptures seriously.

Meanwhile, the scientific and research communities rigorously continue the investigation of human origin. We must understand that these communities are as earnest and zealous in finding and verifying human etiology as are those who practice the presence of the Creator in the story of creation. Our goal as a community of believers should be to look for areas of agreement that do not water down our doctrine. Unfortunately, there are those among us who would rather reinforce alienation when divergence is in view.

Historically, Genesis has created more controversy than any other book. Divisions exist because of continually redrawn lines of varying interpretations of creation and human development. Too often, churches spend time emphasizing points of divergence. But why not spend some of the time on the points of convergence? In this area, we have done poorly. Take, for example, the *Epic of Gilgamesh*.[2] Most evangelicals know little to nothing about the points of convergence between the *Epic of Gilgamesh* and the story of Noah and the flood in Genesis.

When comparing the flood narratives of the biblical account against the *Epic of Gilgamesh*, one notices several divergences. Perhaps the most striking is the purpose of the deities' desire to send the flood. In the Genesis 6–9 account, Yahweh plans to destroy humanity because humans are wicked. In the *Epic of Gilgamesh*, Enlil is more arbitrary: he wants to punish the humans. Enlil plans to do so because the humans have gone astray. Another point of divergence is the way in which humanity is preserved. In Genesis, Yahweh warns Noah to build an ark; while in *Gilgamesh*, it is Ea, a different god, who warns Ut-Napishtim to build a boat. In Genesis,

---

2. Sanders, trans., *Epic of Gilgamesh*.

Identity

Noah brings every species of animal and his immediate family on the ark; while Ut-Napishtim adds skilled craftsmen on his list. In the *Epic of Gilgamesh*, survival is a by-product of human cunning; while in Genesis, survival is purposed in God, as a continuation of creation. Genesis elicits a monotheistic God who has complete control and is omnipotent; while the polytheistic gods of the *Epic of Gilgamesh* do not have complete control of the flood because the one human makes an escape. How much more powerful the Genesis account of our God!

But let us not simply look at the divergences! Let us also consider the similarities. In both accounts, the narratives describe how mankind had become obstinate to their God or gods. In both stories, God and the gods decide to send a worldwide flood. The gods and God know of one righteous man. In the biblical account, this man is Noah; and in the epic, the man is Ut-Napishtim. In both cases, the hero is ordered to create an ark made of wood. In both accounts, the ark is to be covered in pitch. Both accounts have an ark with one door. (Note that in the biblical account, there are two places that mention the samplings of animals. In the first, it is two-by-two; the second mentions seven of each species). Moreover, in both cases the ark is loaded with the hero and samples of animals from across the land. They also share a great rain, and both communicate that the ark landed on a mountain in the Middle East. In both accounts, the hero sends out birds and kills an animal as a ritual sacrifice.

The *Epic of Gilgamesh* is a remarkably similar account of the Noahic flood that we find in scripture. These two ancient stories share about twenty remarkable points of similarity. The point that many of our church's people are oblivious to the *Gilgamesh* account seems suspect to an intelligent nonbeliever. Then, rather than seeing a nonbiblical narrative as an extra-biblical affirmation of the truth of a great flood, nonbelievers see the account as reason for dispute against the human etiology that the Bible claims. In other words, this dispute is an attempt to argue that the authors of the Hebrew Bible (the Torah) simply copied an ancient story about a great flood. This dispute is a distraction. In a study of human origins, the separate accounts of this great flood affirm each other. Together, they make a great case that there was, in fact, a historical flood on the earth.

In a very real sense, our hand is forced to dispute conclusions because of the oversimplified way we treat our own scripture. Instead, let us embrace the richness of the biblical account, such as this, and its relationship to how we interpret our scriptures. Indeed, let us confront the fact that these two narratives are so similar, and in so doing entertain potentially difficult questions about reconciling these stories and the vitality of the inerrancy of scripture. Church leadership must live in the tension, and allow the people of God to live in the tension. The quality of rigor we bring to historical interpretation reveals just how seriously we believe in our own identity.

Technology, Image, and Experience

The church is gripped in a changing media tide. Twitter, Facebook, YouTube, WordPress . . . everything is changing. We limit the message of the gospel when we simply relegate it to written and textual-based teaching. After all, we are moved by these and many other influences. In nearly every way, the battle of how we provide and get information rages.

The written-word and image-based cultures are locked in battle. And, it would seem, the image-based culture is on the verge of victory. This observation leaves us with a great question: What is an adequate response by the church?

One of the areas of church history that I constantly find myself referencing is the iconoclastic controversies of the seventh and eighth centuries. I believe lessons learned by the church during this time period are instructive for us when we consider transitions from a text-based culture to an image-based culture. During this

Identity

time period, two groups battled over whether or not Christians should continue to revere icons (pictures representing a saint, a biblical story, or Christ).[3] Most unsophisticated believers tended to revere icons (iconodules). But many political and religious leaders wanted to have them smashed because they believed veneration of icons to be a form of idolatry (iconoclasts). The iconoclasts saw the use of the icons in worship as idol worship. They pointed to Old Testament prohibitions against images in the Ten Commandments (Exod 20:4). The iconodules counter-argued that icons are not idolatrous because they represent real and alive persons (Christ), whereas idols represented nothing. Moreover, they argued that the spiritual could possess the material. They pointed to the Catholic view of communion and to Christ incarnated. We, as Pentecostals, do not agree with this conclusion in terms of communion, but we can agree in some sense in our use of the handkerchief. (For a biblical example, see Acts 15 for Peter's shadow and the use of handkerchiefs for healing.)

Ultimately, what's really interesting is that the icons stayed. They stayed not because of argument's sake, but owing to something much stronger: societal influence. These icons (later stained glass windows and statues) are visually arresting for the wandering mind of a parishioner during a priest's sermon. These images were created to instruct. They revealed redemption's story. And even though almost all parishioners were illiterate, one could argue that they had a better biblical knowledge base than an average American Christian today.

Still, if a picture is worth a thousand words, then it takes words to describe the picture. This is to say that verbal and written communications will continue to be the two most important and influential means of communication, no matter what sort of media emerge beyond today's latest and greatest. It will be important to work with *descriptive* verbal and written communications, in so doing utilize image in service of that communication. In this way

3. Bettenson, *Documents*, 102.

we can focus the lens through which the larger world will interpret the gospel, our church, and our mission.

Using Film to Inform Theology

Another emerging trend is the use of film to inform a local church's identity and theology. The use of film in a local church has implications from both within and outside its walls. While using film affects the perception of the church in the local community, the greater impact is on church members. I do not mean to decry the use of film, but rather to explore the similarities and differences between the cinema house and a church house. What are the implications for a believing community as it reenacts reality through film, drama, and the like? Contemporary models of church, including the use of image magnification, large video models, and theater seating, show incredible similarities to the philosophical construct of Plato's cave. In all three instances—the church, the cinema, and Plato's allegory of the cave—we see attempts at explaining a grand scheme of the true reality.

Let's take a moment and look at one of philosophy's most important allegories: Plato's "Allegory of the Cave."[4] Imagine that a man is chained to a rock in a cave his whole life. Behind him someone lights a fire, and the chained man begins to see the shadows dancing on the wall. The man perceives these dancing shadows flickering on the wall of the cave to be reality. This perception is precisely the point, according to Plato.

Plato challenges us to break free from the material—to get out of the cave and see the world as it truly exists. It is amazing how relevant his allegory is today. Much like Plato's cave, we subject ourselves to watching images flicker on the back of a theater wall. Note the similarity between his cave and our watching light dance on a wall that is projected by a specialized "fire" inside a projector. These images are used to tell a narrative and, at times,

---

4. Plato, *Republic*, 514–20.

Identity

prompt a discussion of reality. The church, in the same way, uses methods of reality suspension for illustrating ways that its members should use to live more faithfully to a cause. Nonetheless, the church has an understanding between shadow and reality that, at times, is paradoxical.

In church, this suspension is used to help believers focus on the shadow long enough so that they can get a better sense of reality; and yet the church is, in many ways, Plato's cave turned inside-out. The church's conglomerate understanding of shadow and reality is such that it both recognizes the "already-not yet" nature of its existence. In one sense, the church is not merely depicting a shadow of reality that *will be* (i.e., dreams or wishes) but rather one that already exists. The church employs various symbols or images to depict reality, because they represent what is already going on in the community of believers (the kingdom of God), in which believers have access to God through Christ. In another sense, these images represent the "not yet" nature of the kingdom of God. "Not yet" reality is not our present world, but a greater reality that we will see outside the cave. The church literally represents the continual composition of the life tapestry that God the artist is completing until the day of Christ Jesus.

Because of the finite circumstance of corporeal life, the church recognizes the limitations of what it can epistemologically conjure about the nature of reality in narrative form. Many of the greatest Christian thinkers recognized this limitation as it relates to reacting to shadow plays within the cave. Paul recognized this limitation when he said, "Now we see but a poor reflection as in a mirror; then we shall see face to face."[5] Plato locates truth outside the cave, among the stars; whereas, the church finds the truth reflexive, inside the cave. The church understands that when it reenacts shadow plays, such as the life of Christ, it acts with only a portion of the script. That is, the church works with what it is given

5. 1 Cor 13:12, NIV.

within the cave to elucidate what it can about reality, both inside and outside the cave.

While cinema recreates theater as drama, the church is a social construct through which the truth of God is dramatized by way of various rituals and traditions. The church attempts to create both a communal and individual experience in which human ontology is truly captured through the participation of the divine. By proxy, a congregation finds itself through a process of ritualizing its origins, both good and evil. As a result of the larger metanarrative, smaller narratives brought forth through the experience of saints and Scriptures answer the age old Aristotelian question, "What is good?"

In answering these types of questions about possible epistemological answers, the church is very much like the cinema. Cinema, in its attempt to transcend the mundane, ordinary, and normative, produces images that cause viewers to focus intensely on particular objects and symbolic representatives. Through reflection, viewers may be able to understand better what really is or could be. In these ways, cinema mimics the spiritual experience found in church. The difference is that what the church purports really matters.

The church owes at least a part of its theological construction to image. Religious play cycles have dramatized the birth and death of Christ for centuries, and it seems that for many Christians their first thoughts of God and of Christ are associated with image. Often, an introduction to any abstract concept (including an invisible God), requires at least a small anthropomorphic tangibility. (We imagine God using physical human imagery.) This tangibility has taken many forms: Easter plays, Christmas productions, or word pictures through sermon or didactic methodology. The church is unequivocally tied to image in nearly every aspect. Perhaps the difference between church and cinema is simply that in the church image comes more often from the mind's eye rather than from screen to retina to mind.

Identity

The suspension of reality, whether through images or otherwise, is the mobilization of the church. Because film, drama, and play-acting are multisensory (mostly visual), reality suspension through these means are necessary to fulfill the great commission in a local church ministry. Given all the ways humans associate meaning with image, there should be no question that the local church must intentionally utilize these tools for advancing its mission. While the church is like the cinema, the church can maintain its distinction by the way it utilizes film. This requires the church to be steadfast in asking the question of any film: what is the purpose of this film? The same question must be asked of any tool that suspends reality. Going further, leadership must determine how effectively the narrative serves the church's theological purposes. Cinema often uses film as a muse to evoke emotion. Indeed, films are categorized by the particular emotion they are interested in evoking: humor (comedies), love (romances), excitement (thrillers), fright (horror), and more. Frankly, a given film can be utilized in many different ways. That is, a detail in a film's narrative can be used beyond its original intent to explain the greater narrative of the present or future world. However, once a church moves into the realm of using film purely to entertain, amuse, or evoke emotion without any real connection to its mission, or to explain a narrative of reality, it then loses its distinction from the cinema. The church house then becomes the cinema house. More to the point, using film without connection to reality or the mission creates the unintended theological problem of distraction. By using film in this way, a local church condones a loss of focus on the mission. In so doing, the mission itself becomes less critical. Or, put another way, a church like this says, "let's just stay in the cave." To avoid this, a church must maintain the use of film purely for mission fulfillment and reality explanation.

Decentralized Authority and the Greater Need for Community

The greater society today views authority differently than in generations past. Previous generations located authority in leaders of organizations because they respected their titles, and they typically respected the institutions from which those titles emanated. In today's world, the authority of the title has been replaced with the authority of the particular individual. This modern view affects how members of society view the church. In today's world, church members still recognize members of leadership in their official capacity, but they do not recognize the right of a leader to speak into their life from an official title, but through a personal relationship. This is to say, church members are loyal to an individual, not necessarily to the institution. This shift away from institutional loyalty creates unexpected problems. Consider the differences between loyalty as it once was in a Catholic church, and the realities of a Protestant Pentecostal understanding of loyalty.

At Vatican I in 1870, the council of the Roman Catholic Church rallied around an extremely strong organizational hierarchy and set the tone for what had already been a very ritualized and structured style of ecclesiology. Perhaps one of the more infamous outcomes of this council regarded the concept of papal infallibility.[6] This council essentially said that the Pope was infallible in relationship to his morality and also to his teaching, when he taught from his chair. This is called *ex cathedra*, or literally, from the chair. The implication was that the statements the Pope delineated would become church doctrine. This doctrine had a sense of imperativeness—it was to be followed. It is interesting to note that while many staunch Catholics today do not necessarily agree with this theological emanation from Vatican I, they are extremely loyal in their following of Catholic dogma.

---

6. *Decrees of the First Vatican Council*, Session 4, July 18, 1870.

Identity

Now, contrast that loyalty with the conceptual Protestant Pentecostal understanding of the authority of the church. In typical evangelical fashion, the Pentecostal style of theology is gathered around several main faith statements. But beyond that the Pentecostal style leaves much room for theological differences and opinions on a wide variety of issues. The authority of the church and the voice of its leaders are often chosen on style. Like most Free Church models, there is, on occasion, an issue with which the Pentecostal Church takes a position. Nonetheless, these denominational positions have less authority in matters related to the everyday warp and woof of the church. This makes sense if one considers the liquid style of Pentecostal movements. These movements tend to gravitate toward local autonomy, rather than denominational structures. This means that the Pentecostal Church models tend not to standardize educational requirements or specific models. This sensibility is effective for quickly changing ministry environments; but it is dire for reinforcing the authority of the church in matters related to difficult situations. This philosophy also makes it easier for bad teaching to flourish within a local church.

In the early history of the Pentecostal Church, issues of authority were more easily enforced because communities were more close-knit. A pastor's authority directly correlated to the fellowship of his community. Moreover, the people and pastors in a given community networked to create a more accountable church-going public. While these experiences are still true today, our society no longer locates authority in the pastor. Due to the consumerist nature of church-going people, the typical pastor has less authority in the spiritual give and take of people's everyday lives. Other factors in this change include the result of urbanization and secularization. Here's the bottom line: the church-going public simply are not willing to take church discipline seriously. The mere concept is extremely foreign to the church-going public. If a pastor or church leader confronts a situation of sin in an individual's life, the typical response from that individual is to leave that particular local church, or the church universal altogether. This is the nature of the church today.

To remedy problems of institutional authority, it is important to locate local church authority within a set of community practices. Doing so avoids unwarranted perceptions of that church. Using this structure, a local church will not be perceived to have a leader that is a heavy-handed authoritarian; neither will be perceived to have such a loose structure that no one person seems to be in charge. Creating this sort of local church structure also effectively builds community. This community, then, can develop enforceable standards of conduct and discipleship to which members will willingly adhere. That is, members will become loyal to their church institution, and yet will retain personal relationships with church leaders.

To be sure, people will always love a great leader. But great leadership in a community setting means that all members defer to the power of the community. This is why building an authentic community is so important. Such a community creates a safe space for an openness to be who we really are. It also demonstrates to those looking in from the outside that there is genuine care and concern, not superficiality. There is plenty of that elsewhere.

Building community is critical, but it is just one of many steps. We must use this openness as a catalyst for momentum toward personal change. Because of the decentralized approach, accountability now flows from the authority of a communal set of guidelines rather than from the pulpit. We can reinforce communal authority of the saints by having deep-rooted relationships with our church attendees.

IDENTITY FOUND IN COMMUNITY

Paul offers us a wonderful example of building community in a tenuous world. During his correspondence with the church in Corinth (First Corinthians), Paul shows us a church at odds with its founding pastor, Jesus Christ. Sprinkled throughout the entire text of the work are Paul's attempts to offer his credibility as an apostle, as a servant of God, and as one who has authority in matters of spirituality for this particular community. First Corinthians shows how warped expectations can quickly twist into distorted, defined credentials. The church community's relationships should be so rich that those individuals who need discipleship will change their behavior rather than leave the church community.

Nonetheless, modern people are choosing their church. The existential center of this fact creates a practical problem: people with deep spiritual voids are seeking out churches that champion the mentality of a quick fix. In this way we, as a society, as a community, are continually defining our church's identity. At times we are not responsible for these definitions; in other instances we ourselves are responsible, for better or worse.

3

Pastoral Theology in Motion

BELIEF BECOMES behavior. What we think of ourselves, what we believe about our nature and about who God is, eventually result in actions we take. It has been said, "Thoughts lead on to purposes; purposes go forth in action; actions form habits; habits decide character; and character fixes our destiny."[1]

The last chapter focused on the formation of a church's identity as formed by the perceptions and realities of both the believing and non-believing community. Traditional and emerging elements create these theological frameworks of interpretation. This chapter shifts our focus to the theological theories and practices that take place within the world of church leadership. This chapter is not meant to be an extended excursus of systemic theology; rather, this chapter seeks to pinpoint some specific theological concerns for the ministry leaders of our time.

What do we believe about God? That is, what do we believe about our nature and our world? Worldview development is one of the primary roles in the teaching ministry of today's church leader. The theological effects of worldview development not only shape the individuals of the believing community and the people in the world, but they also impact the leader. A worldview is a filter through which one understands and interprets human existence. There are four major elements a worldview can address: human

---

1. Unknown, (although some attribute quote to Tryon Edwards, American theologian).

Pastoral Theology in Motion

origins (etiology), explanation of current status (ontology), morality (ethics), and our human future (futurology or eschatology).[2]

Let's try an example. Look at secular humanism. This worldview begins with a Darwinian etiology. It posits that humanity evolved into its present state from something less than anthropomorphic. Further, secular humanism describes our ontology as one that hasn't evolved past our ancient ideas about race, religion, and deity; thus, our intolerant views toward others remain because of these basic human conceits. As a result, the secular humanist points to the huge role that race and religion has played in wars throughout the centuries. Progress, then, is measured on a societal level, not individually. Morality, in this sense, is not personal. Morality is, rather, about creating a peaceful environment. Because morality can be different for different people, humanity's real moral purpose is to help other peoples and tolerate differences among societies, no matter what. For the secular humanist, the human future is one of two things: continual human progress or some sort of apocalypse that the human race will bring upon itself.

As this example illustrates, a worldview attempts to answer these four elements, either directly or indirectly. This is true with worldview that is secularist, tribal, religious, or a mosaic-like composition. Regardless, a worldview that describes individuals and communities can create either positive or negative outcomes.

All of us pick up some sort of worldview that informs our understanding of the world. Part of this is our brain's continual response to "close the gaps." Throughout life, we have continual background brain activity that attempts to reconcile the total sum of our experiences. This can be an overwhelming experience. It is vital, then, that the mind constantly filter all of its experience through the Scriptures. Failure to do so leaves us open to whatever experience we might have. Without the focused intention of worldview development, theological voids develop. In the following pages we explore theological themes that leaders should apply to their ministry in a world that desperately needs good news.

2. Zacharias, *End of Reason*, 47.

THE LAST DISCIPLE

THE DANGER OF THE THEOLOGICAL VOID

On this dark, cold night in the sandy plain, the wind blows the dust up from the river bend. The dust is carried by the wind in handfuls to a nomadic camp. Many people look for shelter, but do not find it. But inside one tent, warmth and a little light from a candle create a small, safe place. The tent is totally covered, except for a little slit where light shoots out now and then. A woman in a corner lies wet with sweat, sleeping. She is recovering from having just given birth to a baby boy.

The father holds his son proudly, and with as much dignity as a nomadic refugee can muster. Through the howl of driving wind on this cold night, this father makes his voice heard. It is a simple proclamation. "His name will be Bakhut."

Several hours earlier, this family-to-be had been traveling. While in the throes of labor, this mother had agonized her way to this refuge, this last stop at the end of the world. It was a difficult, dangerous, and ruddy road. They traveled on a dehydrated horse, sick from death all around him. All that the beast had wanted was to drink from the one well to which he was brought. But after this nomadic couple spotted the filth decaying in the water, they decided it would be best to let the horse go without water. So there the horse stood on the outside of the tent, parched, its tongue dry in its mouth.

Death, with its incessant flies, was part of the landscape now. Still, this infant was born into nobility, whether it seemed like the kind of nobility one might think of, or not. At one time, this man had owned three hundred sheep and goats, and several horses. As a matter of fact, Bakhut's father used to go to Khartoum, and even used to watch television. But no longer; the Janjaweed, a group of nomadic militants, took all of his sheep and horses. He has nothing now, except his life, his wife, and his son, Bakhut. He takes consolation that he has more than many of the other refugees—a population that was killed or forced from their villages simply because of who they are.

Pastoral Theology in Motion

The passing years bring Bakhut many lessons by the hand of his hardest teacher. This teacher, over time, has taught Bakhut, a boy-turned-man, about the fragile nature of life and the loathing God has for existence. *Experience* is this teacher's name. He experiences the death of his brothers, sisters, and cousins. It is a systematic massacre of his people because of a ruthless dictator who would like nothing more than to wipe his people off the face of the earth. It is a nearly endless march toward death by hunger, thirst, and displacement.

All of Bakhut's behavior flows from his belief in a God who is interested in his capitulation, rather than his well being. Bakhut's alienation from his wife, children, and kinsmen is in part fueled from his hatred of himself, because he believes that God loathes his flesh. After all, God is totally *other*. Bakhut is in no way related to that divine being. No matter what Bakhut does, he feels this sense of fatalistic destiny. For him, it is not a matter of *if* one dies but *how* and *when* one dies. This, because what Bakhut knows about life, he learns from Darfur.

As his kinsmen die around him, Bakhut sizes up the realities of his African heritage and imagines a wonderful land that is full of life. But it's only a fantasy to him, because his understanding of God diminishes the little hope in him. The fact is that his understanding of God is not one of relationship or love. For Bakhut, this world of death is only natural. If only he knew about the God who Paul allows us to see in Eph 3:14–17. If only he knew about the supremacy of a trinitarian community that embraces and sustains true relationships, and that give meaning to life. If only he experienced, in some form, truth that would fly in the face of the suffering around him. Because then he would at least have something other than Darfur as a reference to God.

While this moral narrative is an extreme example, one quickly sees the need for applied theology, or theology in practice. Everywhere, people die on the vine for lack of knowledge. They fail at times because they have no one to teach them a better way.

Still, it is not enough to simply teach one who is absolved. Good theology is theology in motion, theology that is practiced.

Bakhut's reality represents false belief. Although his belief may not change his desperate circumstances, it affects his framework for filtering those circumstances. Regardless of the humanitarian efforts in the face of so much suffering, there can't be true relief without an understanding of a God who is family, who is active in creation, in suffering, in the protest of suffering, and in forgiveness of those who cause suffering. Without that belief, the suffering must appear meaningless. This raises the question: Where are you God?

Where are you? is indeed a question that every human being asks of God, and that God asked of Adam and has asked of every human being since. These are questions that cannot be answered without faith, experience, and reason; and this is why every believer needs a leader. Although anyone can believe what they want about God or the world, the right beliefs aren't always intuitive. The right understanding of God often confronts our own conceptions of the nature of reality and corrects false beliefs about the way the world is.

The mission, then, of every church leader is demonstrating that God is present despite whatever circumstances, good or bad, and that God is actively seeking in us. What active role do you play in piercing the theological void with the full picture of God? Over these next several pages we will see, from a leader's perspective, some antidotes to the void of spiritual darkness. These antidotes include addressing the four elements of a worldview in the terms of pastoral theology. My goal here is to reintroduce you to theological elements that can be integrated into ministry.

In my view, human origin begins theologically in the Trinity. By beginning here we will see that community has always played an inexplicable role in a theology of doing church ministry. In addition, the fall of humanity has significant implications for a theology of the church. Because everyone in a church is fallen,

Pastoral Theology in Motion

our current sinful state affects ministry and creates pitfalls. And so we must address the roots of the fall and its three major effects in the church: isolation, greed, and apathy. We must also revisit the ethical work of Jesus and its implications for mortality. Finally, we must consider how our view of the future affects the mission of the church.

#1 The Trinity in Pastoral Ministry

For this reason I kneel before the Father, from whom his whole family in heaven and on earth derives its name. I pray that out of his glorious riches he may strengthen you with power through his Spirit in your inner being, so that Christ may dwell in your hearts through faith.

EPHESIANS 3:14–17 (NIV)

In this ornately constructed Scripture, Paul plays on words when he uses *Father* and *family*. In the original language, the word for *Father* in the first verse is *Pater* (as in Pater Noster—Our Father), and the word for *family* is *patria*, which is a derivative of *Father*. Paul is saying, in effect, "Look, *family* comes from *Father*." Paul's word game is theologically rich. We can see directly how both saints who have died and gone on, as well as those still on earth, are derived *from him* and are part *of him*. In this text, this "family" language is further developed with the closeness of the other members of the Trinity. This is a rare place in the New Testament because all three members of the Trinity are explicitly woven together. Of course, the Trinity is implicitly prevalent throughout the New Testament, but the word *Trinity* is never part of New Testament language. Still, the Trinity is a vital part of our church belief.

A solid pastoral theology is where religious belief, tradition, and practice meet contemporary questions and experiences. And so, every once in a while, I like to read from the Nicene Creed in our Pentecostal churches and, on occasion, I receive criticism for it. I am told, "Dave, we are not a 'creed' church. We are Pentecostal." Then I always ask one question: "Do you believe in the Trinity?" Inevitably, the answer is a strong "Yes." Then I show my questioner that the doctrine of the Trinity comes from the Nicene council of the church. I do so because it is my firm belief that the Chalcedonian formula is a barometer for understanding who is part of the kingdom. In addition to thoughts on the Trinity, the Chalcedonian formula is "the theological conclusion of the Ecumenical Council held in Chalcedon (451 AD), which attempted to delineate the relationship between Christ's humanity and his deity. The church accepted this as the orthodox statement about the person of Christ."[3] This time-tested piece of church doctrine guards against the influence of Americanized christological cults, such as Mormonism, and also gives us a good understanding of how Christian denominations, in general, are a part of the flock of God.

The Triune God provides uniqueness to our Christian faith, and gives us an inclusive approach to both like-faith and a tool for distinguishing those who have not come to faith. The Trinitarian doctrine is the Christian Church's belief that Father, Son, and Holy Spirit are three Persons in one Godhead. They share the same essence or substance (Greek *homoousios*). Yet, they are three "persons" (Latin *personae*). How the Trinity acts within the world is often called its economy.

The theological construct of the economic Trinity comes from the church fathers Hippolytus and Tertullian. Economy comes from the Greek word *oikonomas*, which in this instance is understood not in financial terms but as household actions that are necessary for living. The word is derived from *oikos*, which means house. In the ancient world, the basic building block of economic vitality and strength was the production per household. This production included servants, animals, family, and the patriarch over the home. In relation to the economic Trinity, each Person

---

3. *Pocket Dictionary of Theological Terms*, 24.

is different and distinct in their manifestation. We are referring to how each acts within the process of creation, regeneration, and everyday matters of life.

Understanding the nature of the Trinity informs our ministry. The doctrine of the Trinity is predicated on the assumption that participation in the Triune God affects our images of who God is in the world, and how his Godself acts. This, of course, also informs our actions.

The Trinity is not three personal realities in isolation from each other. Rather, the Trinity is three Persons in relationality, and they always interweave each other. An ancient word for describing this divine interweaving is *perichoresis*. This term expresses the permeation of each person in the Trinity by the other. They exist in coherence and without confusion. For example, in the Gospel of John, Jesus says, "I am in the Father and the Father is in me," (John 14:11). We understand the Trinity in an intimate communion where the divine partners—the Father, Son, and Holy Spirit—move in and through one another. When we speak of the Triune God, we are not trying to splice one from the other—that would simply damage our understanding of God's nature. Rather, we are exploring the flow of the relationship between them.

One major aspect of pastoral theology and practice in church is prayer. How we pray is related to how we understand the activity of God within the world. The intimate union, mutual indwelling, and even interpenetrating aspects of the three members of the Trinity inform our understanding of prayer. Intercessory prayer is an experience of connection and mutuality with God. When we see God as Triune, we begin to see that even God does not exist in isolation, but within community. When we pray, in some sense we join in this intimate union and mutual indwelling with the Father, Son, and Spirit. Here, God's action is at work in the inner world of human consciousness. Moreover, as created, we have participation with the Creator in divine action. This is amazing! God allows us to participate in the spirituality of others through prayer. We become part of this divine action with God. We must be clear that this is a mystery; but this is, in some sense, persuasion—where intercession becomes the unfolding of a person in the currents of God's love in the world—regardless of whether that individual is a believer or an unbeliever.

Another aspect of pastoral theology and ministry is dealing with theodicy—that is the problem of evil and the results of suffering due to the effects of sin. That God exists in three members allows for the God who suffers and, simultaneously, the God who protests against the injustice of suffering. God's ability to do both simultaneously is accounted through the concept of duality. Duality in the Trinity is represented by opposing capabilities: non-suffering and suffering, detachment and involvement.[4] As Augustine points out, God is impassible in his essence, but becomes passable in Christ. The Father suffers as his children are suffering. *He is suffering with us.* The Son is a person of identification; *he suffers as we suffer.* Finally, the Spirit suffers at the basic depth of unimaginable human life—*in us.*

The Trinity in pastoral theology also offers the ability to look at God through the lens of forgiveness. We interact often with people who need forgiveness and with those who feel like they simply cannot forgive. In this sense, Christ is viewed as an atoning sacrifice who pardons sin through his work on the cross. Nonetheless, the experience for both parties—the one who forgives and the one who is forgiven—is a redemptive exercise. A person who has walked the road of forgiveness and is able to forgive understands that he or she must win an offender to himself or herself. God understands best how to offer forgiveness, due to his direct experience of humanity. The uniqueness of each person of the Trinity, in both the incarnation and the resurrection, is remarkable. Given the nature of God's immutability, reconciling the physical death of one member of the Trinity and the others' response to this action within the community of Godself is an exercise in deep contem-

---

4. Fiddes, *Participating in God*, 234.

plation. This single act of God, within a moment of human history, not only changes humanity's ability to access God but also God's access to humanity.

#2 The Fall of Humanity in Ministry

But God did say, "You must not eat fruit from the tree [of knowledge]⁵ that is in the middle of the garden, and you must not touch it, or you will die"... Then both of their eyes were open and they realized they were naked... But the Lord God called out to the man, "Where are you?" He answered, "I heard you in the garden, and I was afraid because I was naked; so I hid."

GENESIS 3:3, 7, 9–10 (NIV)

When we reflect on the account of the fall of humanity, it is interesting to notice that although Adam and Eve knew that the tree of knowledge of good and evil was "bad" to eat from (and considered "good" not to eat from), they did it anyway. Listen to Eve's words again: "God did say, 'You must not eat fruit from the tree that is in the middle of the garden.'"

This shows that the very thing by which they were tempted (this idea of getting knowledge) wasn't really an issue of seeking knowledge in the first place. They already had the knowledge of eating the fruit. They knew it was evil to eat the fruit, and good not to eat it. Thus, the fall is about their resolve to be obedient to what God had spoken.

The word *yada* (Hebrew), or *know*, plays an important role in this context. Look at what the serpent has said, "For God knows that when you eat of it your eyes will be opened, and you will be like God, knowing good and evil" (Gen 3:5). *Yada* is the word in this phrase, "knowing good and evil"—it means to know experientially. Understand that this isn't head knowledge, but rather to

5. Author's emphasis.

know because of having an experience. Adam and Eve do not have this "knowledge" until they touch the fruit. *Yada* is used in other places in Scripture, such as when referring to a man knowing a woman—idiosyncratic speech, meaning that a man had sexual intimacy with a woman.

In the account of Adam and Eve, it is the act of touching the fruit itself that results in death, as God said, "You will surely die." The touching is prohibited because the action is lethal. It is, in this case, not knowledge of evil but the experiencing of evil for the first time that will result in death. Adam and Eve eat the forbidden fruit. They then realize they are wearing their birthday suits, and it's not even their birthday. This is part of human etiology—the nature of why the world is like it is. Look at the immediate consequences. For the man, it means work will be more difficult. For the woman, birth pains will increase. For the serpent, the results include the loss of communication and the necessity to crawl on the ground. But the agent changed most by the fall is God himself. The intensity of intimacy between God and man is forever changed upon the earth. In the following sections we explore some results of the fall.

Roots of the Fall

Several common pitfalls exist in understanding the origin of the fall. The two most extreme include the following:

- The notion that our original parents merely fell short of the extreme rigor of God upon them.
- That Adam and Eve, in their innocence and ignorance, gained a rising consciousness about the realness of the world.

The latter is a little more sinister than the former because it interprets the fall as being an upward movement of humanity. It engenders the idea that Adam and Eve came to grow and mature to a level of self-assertion and, in so doing, began to make choices about the nature of reality.

Pastoral Theology in Motion

Of course, we can conjecture about the ecology and the genetic predispositions to make an error. We can argue about who is to blame for the fall, which invariably brings up the ad nauseam masculine croak about how it was the woman's fault in the first place. Conversely, we may think, "Well, if I had been in Adam or Eve's place, and known the gravity of the situation and the Pandora's box it would open, I would not have made the same mistake." These fantastic and fatalistic ways of thinking about the nature of the fall are frustrating exercises in futility because, at the end of the day, they are all saying the same thing: "I knew better, but I did it anyway."

In the end, even given the nature of our pride and arrogance, we all believe that Adam and Eve represent us very well. They are, if nothing else, our representatives in this world. They are our representatives in relationship to how they fell. How did they fall? A mixture of unbelief and pride.

Again, epistemology, or know-ability, is about taking responsibility for what we know, and that we are responsible for finding out about what we should know. We are, however, not ethically responsible for what we do not need to know or cannot know. It is often the case that what we know about our universe will translate to an ethical treatment of people, creation, and life in general. What are we supposed to know about our universe? About the earth? What are we supposed to know about God? What should we know about good? About the nature of evil? Or simply what can we know? These questions often spin around the use of knowledge or, to use a modern word, *education*. Education triggers concepts like the use of reason, deduction, and the scientific method. But another word they should trigger is *belief*. Imagine how Bakhut's loathing of God would change if someone would give him a different framework to start with. He would still have to believe it, but his conclusions about God could change.

The foundational point for gaining knowledge is belief. Belief dictates what we can know or understand. It is a subtle but necessary foundation for teaching someone. To know anything, you must first believe something. You must have a starting premise in order to arrive at a conclusion. You simply cannot deduce that 20 × 20 = 400 until you believe that 2 × 2 = 4. The character designation of *two* (2) is a unitary measurement based on many years of history. This has come about through contextualization. Words achieve their denotative connotation and meaning through the continual reaffirmation of understood context.[6] Because the numeral 2 has, over the centuries, achieved a systematic and quantitative empirical proof for the combination of one item and one item, it has been ascribed a concrete value. Thus, the process of memorization of one's multiplication tables reinforces this understood measurement guide. But, at the end of the day, you must believe that 2 × 2 = 4, or you will arrive at a conclusion that is contrary to our common historical system of measure. It is your belief or faith in 2 that makes 2 × 2 = 4. Whether it's your faith in the tradition of the Arabic numerical system, mathematics, or simply faith in the authority of your teacher, the bottom line is that you believe it.

Eve's and, consequentially, Adam's disobedience came as the result of unbelief. They stopped believing that what God said was true. Notice that the serpent opens the door for doubt not once but twice in his conversation with Eve by suggesting, "Did God really say, 'You must not eat from any tree in the garden?'" Eve rebuffs his first morsel of doubt by restating God's command. The serpent then takes a more blatant approach by rejecting God's statement, reversing it, and saying, "Surely you won't die!" Eve existentially begins to prefer her own idea about God's commands. Marguerite Shuster points this out in her assessment of the fall: "Disobedience means one prefers one's own way to God's. Pride means one prefers one's own glory to God's. Unbelief means one prefers one's own understanding to God's."[7] In the end, it is unbelief from which sin enters the world. Unbelief commonly manifests itself as a father from which many other sins spring.

6. Kenny, *Wittgenstein Reader*, 128.
7. Shuster, *Fall and Sin*, 104.

Pastoral Theology in Motion

THE EFFECTS OF THE FALL IN THE LIFE OF THE CHURCH

While both the effects and the nature of the fall can be seen clearly in the world, it is also not absent, nor is it influenced, by the church (an ontological consideration). As stated, the church of Jesus Christ is anthropological in its influence. The church is humanity. Humanity is the church. Is the church pre-fall or post-fall? That is, is the church—a Spirit-birthed, necessary, and redemptive result of the fall—created by God as an agent? Or is the church simply a phenomenon of God's Spirit that existed pre-fall in a community between Adam and Eve, and God? Is the church the entirety of the kingdom? If so, then the church is the agent for the kingdom's influence. This is an interesting discussion that goes beyond the scope of this book. However, in the following pages, we will talk about some possibilities.

I'm going to be arguing for a mixed model. In this model, there is a convergence of the collection of local churches worldwide and the kingdom. Where these two intersect, the effect is redemptive. This, of course, reveals a very wide view of the kingdom. I simply believe that the kingdom has a level of mystery to it. It is larger than we think, and in places that we wouldn't expect. Jesus talks about the kingdom in terms of the way it can be hidden (mustard seed, or a pearl of great price); or it can pop out, like a sudden surprise: it is "among us."[8]

Honest and candid reflection about the true nature of the church worldwide and the kingdom show that the fall has not been without effect. There exist, after all, church structures whose purpose has faded and whose redemptive agency has been lost. Furthermore, as a result of the effects of the fall, the church cannot fully embody the kingdom, collectively. But where it does, the salvific work of God occurs: Redemption through Jesus Christ is where the kingdom and the church come together. When this happens, a community occurs whose cultural pinnacle is the embodied truths of Jesus. It is a kingdom of people whose attitude is

8. Luke 17:21, ISV.

like Jesus. Everything about the individuals change: what they purchase, what they wear, what they want out of life—all of it changes. The fact of the matter is this: where the church and the kingdom meet is never a place, but a condition, given by grace and sanctified by God.

One can come to different conclusions why the effects of the fall are in the physical church. Perhaps an aspect of a local church is that it fails to completely embody the elements of love, peace, and justice that accompany the "inaugurated eschatology"[9] of Jesus' coming. Perhaps a church has been so influenced by the larger culture that its core kerugma has been compromised. Regardless of why the effects are present, my purpose alerts you to them, and will help you ascertain how you can construct a solid, practical theology that recognizes the need to protect against these elements.

A. *Isolationism*

One of the goals of the church is to be unified. Unity in the body of Christ is an essential aspect in the life of the church. A vivid consciousness belongs throughout the church. Friar Georges Florovsky puts it this way, "No Christian is an individual. One Christian is no Christian. The way to God is through our neighbor."[10] Because unity is one of the goals of the Spirit, our enemy's ally is alienation. Because the effects of sin include separation from intimacy with divinity and humanity, the residual effect within the church is isolationism. Isolationism manifests within a variety of ways. First, the continual fragmentation of church denominations shows the work of the enemy. Divide and conquer is the enemy's game.

One of the often overlooked aspects of the Protestant Reformation was Martin Luther's belief that the Catholic Church

---

9. For further reading on this topic see: Ladd, *Presence of the Future* or Wright, *Surprised by Hope*.

10. Kärkkäinen, "SystematicTheology III, Ecclesiology and Eschatology" (lecture, Fuller Theological Seminary, Pasadena, CA, March 2006).

Pastoral Theology in Motion

could be reformed from within. Any good student will reveal that Luther was often frustrated with the peasants' twist of his words to meet their own ends. Our own recent history shows that the value of independence in church life is a strong value of the American church. One of the most important values America's culture contributes to "folk Christianity" is independence. It is a national experiment that has resulted in extreme individualism that, ironically, craves less and less personal accountability. By this I mean that individuals in our culture want freedom from responsibility, on our own terms. The reality is that independence is hardly predicated from a biblical worldview. On the contrary, we are tasked to become so dependent that we are almost like a child in our faith to God.

Indeed, the Scriptures are chock full of warnings against individual isolation. Chapter 6 of Galatians implores us to "carry each other's burdens and fulfill the law of Christ." In the book of James we are instructed to "confess your sins to one another."[11] Without doubt, some of the most powerful times in the Spirit are when the church experiences the mutual edification by its people. It is the "secret" in those "secret sins" that has created bondage, as much as the sin itself. Sin in the church is often directed toward individuality and isolationism. These include sins of inequality and favoritism. The complexity of how isolationism can rear its head is astounding. In some places, it manifests as the failure to see the validity of female leadership in congregational life. We omit fifty percent of God-ordained ministry in the local church if we exclude women from taking their places of edification within the body of Christ. In other instances, the result of isolation is the favoring of some individuals over others. This can be expressed in terms of finances, style, race, or even age. This favoritism is nothing more than the result of isolationism that, in turn, merely serves to disengage some members of the body of Christ. The effects of isolation can

---

11. Gal 6:1 and Jas 5:16, NIV.

come subtly and are even encouraged in some congregations. How we treat the smallest of these effects is no small thing to God.

When we begin down this road, remember that the fall of man begins with food, that the Lord's Supper is for all the saints, and that the conclusion of the age ends with a banquet. The author of James picks this up when he recounts the fact that God does not show favoritism at his table. (See James 2.) The food table is a demonstration of equality. We must once again see that the Trinity embodies a community in unity and in variety. If the Trinity is our theological blueprint for community, then we must be vigilant in creating community that values the duality of uniqueness and unity in the local church. Indeed the local assembly's ecclesial distinction is predicated on unity.

Isolationism also occurs when the church fails to adequately address, misrepresents, or caricatures human sexuality. One thing is clear about human sexuality: it is a difficult aspect of modern church life. But difficulty does not abdicate responsibility; that is, the church is responsible to do more than simply educate and inform its members of what it means to be created in the image of God as a sexual being. The church must also offer meaning in terms of sex. Churches can approach the subject of human sexuality in many different manners. But churches that fail to adequately address human sexuality leave a void that will be filled by many other voices. American culture is obsessed with sexuality because its citizens have a deep desire for intimacy. There is nothing wrong with a desire for intimacy. But there is something wrong with a culture that continually moves toward the taboo and bodily perversion. We devalue ourselves when we deface the image of God upon us. It is like spray painting graffiti on a masterpiece. And when the uniqueness and nobility of our humanity is reduced to its lowest common denominators, then isolation and deep psychosomatic grief result. Our culture's fascination with sexuality requires a church response.

B. Greed

The prosperity movement, which has gained momentum over the last sixty years, is perhaps the most unfortunate turn of events in the church. Only in America can the people of God take seriously some of the ridiculous claims that have been purported from Scripture. I do not think it at all dubious for some of God's people to be extremely blessed. Still, lavishness can easily betray itself. The great Catholic theologian Thomas Aquinas described greed as "Mammon being carried up from Hell by a wolf, coming to inflame the human heart."[12] The desire for an individual to acquire wealth and possession beyond the needs of oneself, especially when the result is the lack or denial of those resources for another, indicates that that individual has little compassion or care. Laissez-faire capitalists will at times argue that greed is not always a negative trait because it creates opportunity for purchasing power. Nonetheless, greed betrays that we do not believe or trust in God as a provider. It is also a betrayal of our community in that we are hoarding resources for ourselves. Our fallen nature is expressed in some very unfortunate ways.

A recent investigation proves that the church is not absent from greed. Senator Charles Grassley, who is one of the top Republicans on the Senate Finance Committee, launched a financial investigation into the lives of six popular television evangelists. Most of these ministry leaders were cooperative, but some of them flatly refused to cooperate. Many of these ministry individuals are great leaders, but the mere existence of this investigation shows that individual greed may hurt the church as a whole, and in the long run. Whatever the result of this investigation, these leaders now have tainted witnesses. Greed can blind.

Typically though, greed works oppositely in the church. That is, members withhold tithes. Perhaps a church member disagrees with the pastor over a particular matter, and so punishes the church by not tithing. Whatever the reasons, we don't hear about

12. Aquinas, *Summa Theologica*.

this sort of greed because it doesn't create a big story. The fact of the matter is that the Biblical principal of tithing supersedes relational problems. The first tenth of one's possessions belong to the Lord. Ron Sider has studied giving trends throughout the evangelical world. He discovered that American Evangelicals, on average, gave approximately 3.6 percent of their income in the 1960s. He also discovered that this percentage of income declined over the years, such that it is around 2.4 percent today.[13] And yet, despite the trend, there exist gems who have learned how to live simply enough to give away 60 percent of their income.

While evangelical giving has never been so dismal, the needs of the world have never been as great as they are today. God has entrusted us to meet needs with the same response as the Savior—who transcends culture to meet the needs of those on the fringe. The outcast, the overlooked, the downtrodden, those facing starvation and disease—it is here where we can find Jesus. Tony Campolo is famous for helping us understand that the poor are sacramental. Campolo reminds us that there is a sense of the sacred in the poor, because when we look at them we have an awareness that Jesus is looking back at us.

C. Apathy

In the violent and plot-twisting movie "The Usual Suspects," Kevin Spacey's character is questioned by the district attorney about a very evil suspect he says disappeared. Spacey says, "The greatest thing the devil ever did was convince the world he doesn't exist." As Spacey's character walks out of the DA's office and into his car, he transforms into the devil who he had described . . . and then he's gone.

One could tell a similar story about our church today. That is, we have convinced ourselves that the world of spirit and supernatural does not exist. Despite the fact that we have fought tooth and nail against a naturalist worldview, we are only willing to go so

---

13. Sider, *Rich Christians*, 65.

far. After all, we don't want to be accused of being hyper-spiritual. Moreover, given the extreme amounts of time Americans spend eating and entertaining, there is little time to think about global needs, much less a ministry that professes to consider the needs of one's neighbor. This is our apathy showing through the cracks in our church buildings.

Apathy, or *apathos*, means to have little feeling or to be passionless. Its counter-opposite is *pathos*, the Greek word meaning full of passion. Dietrich Bonhoffer is noted as saying that the word *church* "to Protestants has the sound of something infinitely commonplace, more or less indifferent and superfluous, that does not make their heart beat faster; something with which a sense of boredom is so often associated."[14] All of this boils down to indifference—and is a part of the new reality of a postmodern culture in general, but also pervades the church of Christ. Our culture, as a whole, is one that values information simply for the sake of information. This is part of an education culture. What results is an information-overfed, under-challenged culture. But information is not action.

It is crucial that we get our church members out of their pews to engage in conversation, engage in plans, and engage in places of ministry. Apathy can be quickly overcome in the short term. Indeed, apathetic people will act generously toward the dispossessed in times of great trouble—a nationwide outpouring of generosity after a natural disaster is proof of this. However, extending that response long-term requires a great effort. When people come to a place where they truly are intimate with God, the result is incredible action. Intimacy fuels their understanding that a deeper way to God is through others. Deep service to another creates solidarity between the created and the creator, because we begin to embody God's truest nature: humility.

Apathy is also caused by unbelief. In a church setting, this is usually caused by a sense of civil religion in society. We believe

---

14. Neuhaus, *Catholic Matters*, 37.

in God to the degree and extent that God is a help to us when we are in trouble. Other than that, we are in church because we have a sense of duty to our Christian tradition. What a waste! God is interested in a people who will trust him with their entire being. Most people spend a large amount of time in the pew waiting on God to speak to them about his will, so they can consider it with all their options, and then make a decision. This waiting game also can lead to apathy.

God does not play this type of game. God does not give direction to a church interested in considering what he would do if he were in their shoes. When God speaks, it is not for contemplation, it is for participation. Our churches must proclaim, "Okay, God, we care what you say! Our response will be obedience. Yes, we will do it." When we reach that point, we receive an incredible amount of communication from God. A church that overcomes apathy in this way will receive guidance for its next steps in life. This is theology in motion!

#3 Christian Ethics and Morality

Despite our fallen nature, we must find ways to follow Jesus. Jesus created a work of ethics that is informative and perfect in theorization and implementation. Quite simply, we have to take seriously the life and words of Jesus. Let us consider the life of Jesus and his crowning work, the Sermon on the Mount. When Jesus says that we have to love our enemies, it must be taken to heart and implemented. When we read in Matt 5:3 that "the poor in Spirit are blessed," some of us must take vows to be poor for his blessing. This doesn't necessarily mean taking a vow of poverty for poverty's sake, but rather developing a willingness to commit to that which God calls us, regardless of the amount of financial remuneration.

These words are easier read than done, of course. We are fallen. But this fact does not absolve us. For assistance in putting the words of Jesus into action, it is helpful to look at the initiatives

Jesus communicated in his great sermon as guidelines that inform the teachings of the Old Testament. Jesus preached more on the kingdom of God than any other topic. Moreover, the Sermon on the Mount, which is Jesus' largest and most focused teaching, Jesus concerned himself with the elements of this kingdom. And yet, we fail to include systematic and engaged teaching in this theological vein.

This raises the question as to why we in the American church culture have glossed over the largest body of Jesus' communication to humanity. I believe there are a few key reasons. The first stems from the nature of our interpretive communities. Unfortunately, we have backed away from our rich history, which includes Christ's difficult lessons about love for one's enemies and clear indicative for reconciliation. Instead, we have allowed the American church culture and nationalism to supplant a serious look at Christ's claims. The second reason for this glossing over of Christ's message is a product of a hermeneutic of the Sermon on the Mount in our communities of faith. We have either set aside notions of unattainable perfectionism for those who are in leadership, or we have inadvertently taken the viewpoint of Luther, who took a dualistic view of the Sermon on the Mount in his "Theology of Two Realms." In the latter case, the Sermon on the Mount is viewed as a teaching for a Christian's attitude. Simply, its messages should be considered, but they should not be applied to our actions, nor should they be applied to the actions of the authorities of the world. Luther created this viewpoint because he wanted to make sure he didn't create a reason for people to be insubordinate to the authority placed over them.

The end result of this dualistic approach is a dichotomy of the sacred and the secular. It is here we can pinpoint the literal beginnings of secularization. As with most destructive ideologies against the gospel, secularism comes not from the outside of the church, but from inside. Luther did incredible things to advance the Church, but his good works also created deleterious side effects. In this case, we in the American church culture have ascribed to Luther's teachings. We have relegated the Sermon on the Mount to the inner workings of a person's heart; and in so doing have divorced its real-world application for biblical social justice or its attempts to make the world better through faith initiatives. The result is that non-Christians, with a deep sense of justice, look at Christians and say to themselves, "What frauds!"

Be assured that following what Jesus says will be counter-culture. My hope is that we, as Pentecostals, will reexamine Jesus' teaching on justice, to the extent that we can again reach the implications that were reached by Augustine, Aquinas, and the early Pentecostals. These examinations resulted in the development of a justice war theology. On this particular topic alone, the early Pentecostals were so counter-culture that they were pacifistic. How far we have come! Personally speaking, I am not a pacifist. But in my call to reexamine the claims of Christ, it has become clear to me that we have often simply taken up a nationalist ideology because it's the path of least resistance. This is to say, without the guidance of Christ, our people become a feather in the wind without a theological point of anchor. Our people therefore cannot choose a theological reason for action. Rather, they allow nationalism to dictate their theology for them.

Let us work through some of the Sermon on the Mount. We will begin in chapter 5 of Matthew, which starts with the Beatitudes. The word *beatitude* comes from the Latin word *beatus*. *Beatus*, essentially, can be translated into *blessing*. This type of blessing didactic would have been a relatively common form in Christ's day. Moreover, Christ's listeners would have been familiar with the genre due to the myriad examples of blessings and curses found in the works of the prophets. Although the style would have been familiar to them, the content would have not. In a very real sense, these teachings were and remain counter-cultural in a way that is almost shocking in their explanation.

Pastoral Theology in Motion

Blessed are the poor in spirit, for theirs is the kingdom of heaven.
Blessed are those who mourn, for they will be comforted.
Blessed are the meek, for they will inherit the earth.
Blessed are those who hunger and thirst for righteousness, for they will be filled.
Blessed are the merciful, for they will be shown mercy.
Blessed are the pure in heart, for they will see God.
Blessed are the peacemakers, for they will be called sons of God.
Blessed are those who are persecuted because of righteousness, for theirs is the kingdom of heaven.
MATTHEW 5:3–10 (NIV)

The verdict is still out on whether or not Jesus is describing the characteristics of his current followers, or if this is what his followers must do in the future. Regardless, it is clear that these are characteristics of people who are heirs of the kingdom of God. The person who is "poor in spirit" understands the reality of humanity in light of a God who is perfect. The paradox of the kingdom of God, something I like to call the *law of spiritual reciprocity*, is at work here too. Here are some examples of spiritual reciprocity:

- We get by giving it away.
- We find by losing.
- We are whole by being broken before God.
- We live by dying.
- We succeed by rising from the ashes of supreme sacrifice.

Notions of spiritual reciprocity also include mourning, meekness, mercy, and peacemaking.

Those who follow the law of spiritual reciprocity ultimately get what their heart desires. If you really want to have mercy, give it away to others. Those who hunger for God truly and legitimately get what their heart desires, for they will see him. Of course, the converse can also be inferred. Those who simply want God because of what he can do for them will also get what they want, but they may discover they desired wrongly.

After the Beatitudes, Jesus moves into a short teaching on the importance of the people of God to be salt and light, as well as to announce that he has come to fulfill the law. Then he launches into the full-blown teaching on perennial issues, ways people can get trapped in committing the sins associated with them, and how to escape having to commit them.

Among many teachings, I have found regarding this last portion of the Sermon of the Mount, *Kingdom Ethics* by Glen Stassen and David Gushee is an excellent resource.[15] They show how Jesus used a pattern of a triad in teaching transforming initiatives. The triad starts with the traditional teaching on righteousness, usually with Jesus' words, "You have heard it said . . ." Then, the pattern switches to the cycle that may result from following the law without Jesus' transforming initiative. This is usually marked with Jesus' words, "But I say to you . . ." The final portion, then, is Jesus' transformational teaching. It is here where he moves beyond the traditional behavior to the spirit of the Old Testament teaching. Following these teachings, time and again, Jesus calls for reconciliation and self-sacrifice, rather than self-protection or self-preservation. In the case of murder and anger, he calls for the apposition. De-escalation in the opposite direction creates friendships out of animosity. Following these hard teachings of Jesus require deep humility and loss of self-aggrandizement. Without these elements, the practice of Christian ethics will not take place.

#4 The Future and the Church's Mission

Regardless of your thoughts on eschatology, it permeates Scripture. Rather than focus on eschatological schools, let's take a broad view of the future in general and the local church in particular. Every church leader must come to grips with the primary message of

---

15. Stassen, *Kingdom Ethics*, 125–45.

Jesus: The kingdom of God is at hand. His message was of the imminent kingdom of God. Without coming to grips with the *immanency* of that kingdom, church leaders will neither capture the kingdom itself nor will you understand what I am about to say.

The nature of the kingdom itself is future-as-present. I tend to agree with contemporary theologian Wolfhart Pannenberg that the present and the future are actually interwoven.[16] This has implications for our etiology, ontology, and mortality. Christ not only lived in a hope he created but, because of him, Christianity, and subsequently your local church, is oriented toward the future. That future hope should drive the ministry of each church leader. The future is those events not yet occurring but will occur. This is because of the acts that are predicated on God's existence are ahead of us. In that sense, God is not only near to us and far from us but also before us in time. Only can the unity in the Trinity account for the centripetality of all reality. And, by the way, the kingdom is expanding as the universe and future expand. See Colossians 1.

The scriptures demonstrate the future nature of the kingdom. It teaches us that God has been working ahead of us. Our future, our God, is there for those who wish to see him. From Abraham to Peter, the scriptures paint a picture of individuals who exchange one life of the past for a future life in community with God. Moreover, the scriptures demonstrate we will continue beyond what we presently know; and in that future we will have a greater sense of meaning of the past. Finally, the scriptures demonstrate that what we do here has consequences in the future. The future is now.

Let me demonstrate where all of this ultimately leads. The Cappadocian Fathers demonstrated that Jesus became flesh so that in the future kingdom we could participate with the divine. The descent of Jesus enables the future humanity to be capable of ascent in relationality with God. How was the descent of Jesus made possible? It was through the power of the Holy Spirit. Charismatic

---

16. Pannenberg, *Theology and the Kingdom of God*, 53.

spirituality and spiritual gifts demonstrate a look toward the future. Pentecost, as a confirmation of the Spirit's presence, signifies the beginning of the future for the church as a community in deep participation with the Trinity.

If the nature of the kingdom is future-as-present, then we are called as leaders to both anticipate and participate in that future through the transformation of our lives and our world. The danger in losing this anticipation means losing what is elemental to ecclesiology. Again, without this understanding of immanency, the suffering of Bakhut in Darfur and what we can do about it is meaningless. Suffering can only find meaning when understood in the context of belief in the future kingdom. We cannot have any sort of purpose in a church model without understanding agency in the imminence of the kingdom. This should drive the church deeper in the active agency of mission in the world. We have a hand in this future by acting in the present.

4

Challenges

THIS CHAPTER explores eight key challenges facing the Pentecostal Church today. These challenges reveal why the church has less of an impact on today's society. By confronting these challenges our church can reform its spiritual life and, in so doing, regain its place of influence in the lives of our families, our congregations, and our larger society.

The first challenge is the result of urbanization. The second challenge is a radical divergence to make disciples. The third challenge is our society's postmodern mindset. The fourth challenge involves retooling our ideas of community, such that we can disciple people who have a postmodern mindset. The fifth challenge requires us to redevelop relational ministries and leadership. The sixth challenge regards our teaching of the origins of Scripture. The seventh challenge asks us to think through how we can eliminate cultural irrelevance. The final challenge—and one of the most difficult—is combating the loss of selflessness in our churches today.

EFFECTS OF URBANIZATION

Urbanization has played a huge role in the disengagement of the church from society today. This disengagement is the result and the continued consequence of the Industrial Revolution. For a variety of economic and social reasons, people from rural communities continue to migrate toward urban centers. With rapid relocation to urban centers, social disruption occurs. With this disruption comes the potential to form new contacts and alliances. The larger city also promotes a level of personal anonymity. People who may have been involved heavily in a church, that itself was a major influence in the landscape of a town, now often find the city church to have a token presence.

So, when these people migrate from a rural to an urban setting, they experience a level of disorientation: what was normative in their small town has been relegated to what would be considered fringe or even counter-culture. People who are not committed to a religious community will eventually find this reorientation unacceptable; and so they assimilate into a secular society simply because it is the most socially acceptable course of action. These people then question whether or not their personal beliefs were really grounded in a biblical framework, or if they had instead experienced a strong group mentality in their former town. Nonetheless, they are lost to the church of Christ.

Urban centers also seem to be strongholds of plurality and secularization. Plurality is due to a large and diverse population. Indeed, it is important for cities to employ and enforce a level of toleration, which is necessary for the freedom of religious and social practices. Nonetheless, secularization relegates religion, and consequently the church, to private life rather than public life.

Secularization is influenced more by materialism than it is to atheism or even secular humanism. While materialism, atheism, and secular humanism have a role influencing change in the public arena, the lowest common denominator is secularization. Atheism and secular humanism are more academic in nature and, thus, are deliberate acts toward the philosophical ideology that is secularity. Materialism, on the other hand, is more an act of omission. That is, omission is less of an intentional or willful response and more of a *lack* of response. The majority of people in urban centers fall into the category of materialism. People have given their lives to *stuff*. Life in an urban center can generally be much more comfortable and luxurious than life in a rural setting. Nonetheless, the cost is higher in an urban setting and, in some sense, you get less for more. This is the pretentious rat race we call city living.

Materialism is so pervasive that it has invaded every aspect of American culture. Documented proof exists to provide correlation between the movement from a Protestant work ethic associated with church life to laisser-faire capitalism: there are entire history books based on this premise. For further reading on this premise see Miller's *The Errand into the Wilderness* and Noll's *A History of Christianity in the United States and* Canada. We, as a culture, have created our own monster. We as a culture need to rediscover the Sabbath and the theological axiom that teaches it is a holy day; and it is made for us to be a day that we find rest.

In the United States, we have documented history that most of the growth of the church in antebellum America came from the mainline denominations from Europe. These Americans were simply plugging immigrants into churches based on language and culture groups. This was the case until after the American Civil War, when pioneers and settlers began to move westward in unprecedented numbers. The mainline denominations such as the Anglican, Presbyterian, and even Lutheran were too large and cumbersome to anticipate and adapt to the changing style of this western expansion. However, the Baptist and Methodist preachers of the period rose to the challenge. Moreover, the Baptist and Methodist movements were relatively young in their denominational existence and so had less bureaucratic restraints. The Methodist circuit rider model capitalized on the fact that he could quickly move from town to town, or at least from preaching point to preaching point. The rough nature of these preachers was welcomed by settlers who were accustomed to a rough style. While these preachers were starting mission churches on the frontier of America, the mainline denominations were still waiting for roads to be made and train tracks to be laid. As a result, these Free Church[1] movements began to explode. The First and Second Great Awakenings under George Whitefield, Jonathan Edwards, and

---

1. A Free Church movement is a denomination that is separated from government or an established state church.

Charles G. Finney provided a second impetus for the growth of these frontier churches. It was a time of explosive growth as frontier populations doubled and tripled. No longer was the growth of churches due to the inherited religious background from Europe, or even by people being born into the church. Church growth was rather, for the first time, truly evangelical in nature.

Of course, some of these frontier towns became urban centers. America's eastern cities grew too. From 1860 to 1960 working people who moved into America's urban centers became our industrial workforce. Family life changed too—no longer intimately connected to the land, families became "rootless." Around 1960, we again experienced a change in our way of life. With the rapid expansion of cities came expensive housing, difficult traffic, and dangerous neighborhoods. To help its citizens escape the rat race pace of city life, yet enjoy its financial solidarity, communities began creating bedroom or satellite communities called *suburbs*. This, once again, destabilized the family unit as the extended family transformed into the nuclear family. Suburbanization was a decentralizing force in the role of a community and church. No longer did people work in the same community in which they lived. There was no single, directional flow of people in and out of communities. Instead, people flowed in completely different rhythms from each other. Decentralization is the keyword we need to take away, here.

A father may travel to an urban center for work and then travel back to his home in suburbia. On the other hand, his wife may be a part of a school board that is zoned within their neighborhood but is actually located in another community. Their son may be involved in sports at his local hangout, which is ten miles from home and located in yet a different community. It would not be uncommon for a family like this to drive thirty miles to visit an entertainment complex.

Urbanization in the American setting has created decentralization. Decentralization, I believe, is the primary reason that the

American family feels disconnected today. While a family today might live in a physical, demographic location, it is likely not a part of a traditional community. It is therefore crucial that our church fill this social void and become a stabilizing community force. Our individual families need a larger community. This cannot be understated. We, as a church, must not overlook this need. Moreover, importance should also be paid to reconnecting individual families within the church setting.

It has been said that American society is most segregated on a Sunday morning. While this is not entirely true, church settings can often separate a family based on age. Age divisions are vital for educational purposes, such as Sunday school or small groups; however, churches that desire authentic community must look for opportunities to reinforce family relationships. Families that are well-connected create stronger churches. Does your church have a family development strategy? Does your program help families feel more equipped to be a family because of your church's service? Or does your program reinforce familial disconnection? What time of your church's weekly schedule intentionally puts the family together? How much time? When does your church coach parenting skills to its fathers or mothers? Does your church even provide such coaching? This is a huge need in our society, and this topic should not simply be marginalized to a Father's Day or Mother's Day sermon. Does your church have a singles' ministry? How you model family and how well you practice family directly affects the health of your church community.

As we have discovered, urbanization creates problems of disconnectedness within families.[2] This disconnectedness exists because of the modern workplace too. People working within corporate structures crave free time by the end of the week. The type of time they are looking for is unstructured, unplanned, and spontaneous. (This is the opposite need of rural folk who, by contrast, want structure.) Urbanities are also looking for solid

2. Gibbs, *In Name Only*, 12.

relationships that are not predicated on agenda or are focused on some sort of need or project. Singles compose the largest group of these urbanites. Churches that want to attract these urban singles must consider the type of contact points they offer. These contact points must be fluid. Participants must be able to easily come and go. These points should not require a large commitment level to the social group. Contact points of these types include coffee shops, restaurants that encourage conversation between strangers, or places that feature activities of common interest, like a sporting event. These informal contact points are much more important for building community than are actual church services. Church services do not build authentic community.

I remember talking with several men at the Village Church in Dallas. We were discussing the relationships that gave them spiritual enrichment and friendship. Where did these entry points in the life of the church come into play? Small groups? A church service? Nope. These entry points were the church's large basketball, baseball, and sports groups. Because the events at these places were not structured or focused on an agenda, these individuals were able to talk about the real-life needs they had. The emotions experienced from some canned curriculum offered little meaningful value to this very typical group of men.

Urbanization Creates Difficult Ministry Groups

It's sad to say that part of our collective identity as a church includes a perpetual ignoring of difficult ministry groups. This denial transcends nearly every denomination, whether evangelical, Reformed, or Catholic. We simply practice our church life as if these certain groups do not exist. We love crowds, but we don't know what to do with people. This shows our lack of sincerity to the people of our society and our society's needs.

For example, more children are born into single-parent families than "typical nuclear" families. Ask yourself this question: when was the last time you saw a curriculum for single-parent children or for single parents? If your answer is never, you're right! It doesn't exist. We are trying to minister to people in broad strokes, rather than to people on individual bases. The good news of the gospel is that it simply isn't for normal people—whoever they are—it's for people of *all walks of life*. We have become a church community that is only good at holding services. This is where we are slowly relegating our ministry. That's not a good sign.

Consider these numbers from the 2009 U.S. census bureau regarding singles and the changing American household: there are 95.7 million unmarried and single Americans. This group comprises 43 percent of all of those over age fifteen. Sixty-three percent of unmarried and single Americans have never been married. Nearly twenty-nine million people in this country live alone. This last number represents 26 percent of all households.[3]

What is your church doing to minister to this group?

A RADICAL DIVERGENCE
TO MAKE DISCIPLES OUT OF CONVERTS

The hiatus that the American Church has taken from its christological mandate to disciple its people takes one's breath away. One goals of this work is to reengage the American Church to its original missional task. In the words of Jesus, this task is "to make disciples." The reengagement of the mission requires us to consider some of the historical moves of the American Church. To do so, we must reflect on a variety of antidotes that are well worth their historical value. These historical accounts provide a framework for seeing how we moved from being authentic disciples of Christ to becoming marginal players in the multicultural world of the United States.

American churches today are filled with undiscipled people. Simply, we have overused a supplemental approach to move peo-

---

3. U.S. Census Bureau. "United States Fact Sheet." American Fact Finder Fact Sheet, 2005–2009. Online: http://factfinder.census.gov/servlet/DatasetMainPageServlet?_program=ACS&_lang=en&_ts=100621288252.

ple into discipleship. I believe that, as a mode of leading a person into the journey of salvation, the practice of praying the sinner's prayer has come and gone. This practice began in the Second Great Awakening two hundred years ago in the tent revivals of Charles G. Finney.[4] His use of the anxious bench produced our modern use of the altar. As a matter of fact, many of our altars look very much like Finney's anxious bench. The use of the sinner's prayer was an effective means of evangelism when Christian thought and theology were part of the greater culture. As our greater culture shifted, we gave our allegiances to theism, neo-theism, and eventually syncretism. Today, the sinner's prayer, or the Lord's Prayer, leaves the pre-discipled convert on the threshing floor of belief. These pre-discipled individuals possess little transformational knowledge, and so they form a conceptual gap between decision and discipleship. This means trouble for this member of Christ!

We must reexamine the invitation to journey. The practice of praying the sinner's prayer is not the appropriate biblical model for our time. Indeed, we must consider a much older form of inquiry into the spiritual crossing into salvation, which is worked out with fear and trembling. "Come and see," Phillip says to Nathaniel. "We have found him. We have found Jesus."[5] Phillip is communicating to Nathaniel a truly biblical mode of invitation to journey, and this is also what Jesus asks of his disciples. He does not simply ask them to pray a salvific prayer; rather, he invites them to follow his lead.

For Paul, conversion was a decision; but for the disciples, it was a journey. Paul's conversion was a journey of the heart because he was already steeped in the "traditions of his Fathers." To the twelve, however, the salvific journey was essential because they did not have nearly the education level of Paul. Theirs was a journey of information, translation, and reformation.

Imagine that the Kingdom of God is like a distant country. When one seeks to enter into it, one must first discover the direc-

---

4. Noll, *History of Christianity*, 176.
5. John 1:43–46 NIV.

tion one must travel to get to its borders. And then, when at the border, one must discover what is required to get in. This is the information gathering. Once past the border, in order to become oriented to this new country one must become immersed in the culture, the language, and the practices of the land. This is the translation. But one doesn't fully inculcate in this distant country until one takes up residence and plants oneself. It is a process that can take years. But, once established, the conversion is complete. This is the reformation. Finally, one could say a person cannot ever truly be a part of this new country unless he or she is born into it. The latter thought represents a belief that hasn't changed in over two thousand years.

The act of baptism aside, many well-educated people sit on the fence about their relationship with God. These are people who need to take a journey of the heart. These are the modern-day Pauls. For the less educated, our modern-day twelve, they need to understand it is not a decision they are making, but rather a journey they are taking.

This raises an important question. What sort of salvific journey does our church demand? The answer is expressed in the quality of the invitation we offer. Simply, we have relegated more and more ministry, in general, to the level of a one-night tent revival. We say, "Let's just get people to accept Jesus." And so we pray the sinner's prayer. But if there is no disciple, there is no Christian. An individual who does nothing more than accept the sinner's prayer has merely given ascent to the idea of Jesus as their Lord.

The quality of church teaching is also problematic. Teaching that represents the life of a Christian as being carefree, with quick gratification and near-guarantee of earthly success, only creates conditions of disillusion and regret among recent converts. I call this the gospel of self-esteem. "You can be a winner, just like me." Thanks, but let's leave this feel-good message to the feel-good psychologists.

We have to recognize that Christian identity can be understood purely as an act of identification with the crucified Christ. The cross as a symbol of defeat before the victory of God is a remarkable tool of discipleship. This cannot be overstated. We are always bearing the marks of Christ, because we are to have fellowship with his suffering and become like him in his death. Jesus' prescription for discipleship expands this very well. The three requirements for discipleship, he says, are self-denial, cross bearing, and followership.[6] Personally, I love the fact that all of these are Greek imperatives; but the last one, especially, seems to be a promise to those abandoned by this world. Jesus is not simply sending us on the journey alone, he is going with us. "Follow me." Thus, when we look at the cross and see that divinely dark moment in the Trinity where the Father turns his back on the Son, we recognize that this act of denial is for us. That the Father excludes the Son in favor of the embrace of humanity is something of an unutterable mystery. His exclusion was for our embrace.

Christ, who identifies himself as one abandoned by his own Father at the moment when he needs him the most, has much to say, theologically, about today's culture. We must disciple our congregations such that they understand that only when one follows the cross and carries the commands of Jesus, will one inherit his life.

UNDERSTANDING POSTMODERN SOCIETY

A postmodern society presents great challenges for a church that desires to regain its cultural influence. We could argue back and forth whether we are postmodernists or depressed modernists.[7] Nonetheless, for the sake of argument, we will fall in with postmodernism. Some would say that postmodernism ought to be celebrated because it marks the end of delusional philosophies and the dissolution of foundational thought. Ultimately, in postmodern

---

6. Luke 9:23 NIV.

7. Murphy, Anglo-American Postmodernity Lecture, Jan. 23, 2006. Murphy argues that we are, currently, depressed modernists.

Challenges

thought there is no direct experience of reality without interpretation; and all interpretation is corrupted at some point by either external or internal forces. The postmodernist would argue that one could not know if they had interpreted their faith correctly. Yet, for the postmodernist, this is not necessarily a problem.

This is why the biblical notion of discipleship is complementary to postmodernism. Amid a sea of doubt in the postmodernist's mind, the possibility of deeply knowing God rises. However, the concept of having a relationship with God is very subjective to them. Most postmodernists would say that a god exists, but that no one knows what kind of god he or she is. As a result, they would say that God is not a knowable being. This is also why we have so many agnostics among us today.

Modernists, especially modern-thinking Christians, would claim that, as one attempts to seek truth, the knowledge gleaned from the search would point the wanderer back toward God. This is the idea that truth is attainable, but just out of reach. The postmodernist would say that although one may accept a "truth," it is true only because the thinker believes the concepts of the truth are true. Therefore, truth is not systematic reasoning, but is the rationale for what one considers to be correct. Essentially postmodern beliefs are emotively and relationally based, rather than rationally and logically based. This is why postmodernists see faith as a correct and viable approach to life, and why some have a respect for the faith upon which the system of Christianity is based.

The potential discipler must understand the underlying philosophy of postmodernism; specifically, that truth is something learned within community. Richard Rorty is one of the foremost thinkers in this area of postmodernism. Rorty's premise is set on the utter failure of epistemology and the history of philosophy.[8] Therefore, Rorty advocates what is called pragmatism. Rorty's pragmatism is linked with his ethnocentrism. Ethnocentrism, according to Rorty, is not racism. Ethnocentrism is the recognition

8. Carson, *Telling the Truth*, 69.

that, in our actual practice, we appeal to, argue with, and take seriously those who share our general take on the world.[9] We justify our beliefs primarily in and to our own communities.

The postmodern understanding of socialization gives its adherents an imperfect view of truth. They see that conformity or group-think happens on some level for the individual, because of imposed cultural norms. They may be charged with overextending this view of truth to indicate that there is no universal or absolute truth. However, this is not an entirely correct portrayal of postmodern understanding. Contrary to some schools of thought, postmodernists do believe that there exists absolute truth—they just do not believe in absolute knowledge.[10] That is, they do not believe in the teacher's ability to apprehend and communicate that truth. A person or group's self-understanding is not to be viewed as a reliable source of knowledge because it was distorted by psychological delusion, perspectival illusion, and ideological prejudice.[11]

According to postmodernists, truths are simply the social contract from which we subsist in a culture. Postmodernists accept the idea of faith because it is non-objective and emotionally based and, therefore, does not threaten the idea of knowability. Rather, the individual chooses the belief that best suits himself or herself, and, quite often, that means filling the need of belonging. The Christian follows the cultural norms that the community agrees on, because, in order for that person to be successful and become a member of a particular subculture, they need to subject themselves to the understanding of the community. On the other side of the issue, postmodernists believe that moral decisions rest on the personal responsibility of the individual, and, because there is no objectivity in knowledge, individuals must rely on their own emotions and beliefs.

The nature of postmodernism moves the seeker of knowledge and potential disciple toward skepticism. Again, many agnostics

9. Ibid., 73.
10. McLaren, *Church on the Other Side*, 166.
11. Freud, *Civilization and Its Discontents*, 256.

walk among us. The seeker has been trained to continuously reevaluate the foundation of knowledge.[12] For Foucault, one of the great postmodern philosophers, truth is not discovered, but fashioned. However, I would disagree with Foucault's idea that no one simply "knows" something. Foucault believed we know something "for" something, and, as such, knowledge is inextricably tied up with power. "Truth isn't outside power... Truth is a thing of this world: it is produced only by virtue of multiple forms of constraint."[13] However, it seems that to know *anything*, you must believe *something*. Even the postmodern seeker has presuppositions, so that they assume some things are true. It is imperative that the discipler exposes those presuppositions. Once these are exposed, the postmodernist can realize that there are specific possibilities they are presupposing and, as a result, are avoiding other possibilities. Ultimately, what the postmodernist wants is not perfect knowledge or truth, but rather freedom from skepticism.

Another aspect of postmodernism is the understanding of linguistics and the nature of reality as it relates to truth. Logical positivist Ludwig Wittgenstein said that, "language was the application of morality."[14] Later, he came to reject this, his own theory of language. He and others have concluded that there will never be a master language. "Words achieve their denotative function only through connotative associations in established usage."[15] Thus, connotation creates the function of the language or word, itself. For example, the metaphor achieves its meaning by holding two words that are opposites in tension, thereby creating a contrast and a new meaning. It is possible to argue that models, symbols, and theories also function as complex metaphors. It is true that words are only unitary symbols for measuring and memorizing in the use of language; although this truth does not rule out their semantic

12. Gross and Levitt, *Higher superstition*, 93.
13. Carson, *Telling the Truth*, 80.
14. Kenny, *Wittgenstein Reader*, 175.
15. Ibid., 128.

meaning. If it did, as many have pointed out, then the claims of postmodernists themselves would be devoid of meaning.

If one can illustrate that words express some truth, and semantic meaning points toward that truth, then one can conclude that a statement has some meaning while paradoxically realizing that our understanding is limited because we ourselves are finite. The postmodern understanding of our finite being relates to the faith, truth, community, and language necessary for discipleship. These understandings present some challenges as well.

RETOOLING DISCIPLESHIP MODELS FOR POSTMODERNISTS

A discipler (pastor, teacher, leader, or believer) must understand that a postmodernist's moral standards are self-chosen. No one is to answer to these morals, except the one moralizing. Rorty quotes Foucault, saying that this is "self-creation," where it is believed that we "create ourselves as a work of art."[16] Any challenge to the person's worldview in the name of Christ will be seen as expressing disparagement of the artist's work. To overcome this way of thinking, a discipler may be required to redevelop the idea of community. That is, the disciples must be led to understand that the community's subsistent belief of truth is not relative. The discipler must demonstrate these community truths by example, and in so doing reinforce his or her teachings.

Disciplers must rise to this challenge. No longer can they make absolute claims. Many disciplers, in a Kantian-like sense, wish to categorically "prove" basic Christian doctrine as a way of attempting to settle skepticism. Unfortunately, this systematic and reactionary behavior is precisely what drives away the potential postmodern disciple. Disciplers must remember that postmodernists seem to have a capacity to endure ambiguity quite calmly

---

16. Carson, *Telling the Truth*, 86.

Challenges

and live with equanimity.[17] Therefore, the discipler should allow questions of faith to be wrestled with, and should not attempt to settle questions with absolute conclusions.

The last and perhaps greatest challenge of discipleship is overcoming the postmodern belief that universal claims or metanarratives are inadmissible. A metanarrative is a story, narrative, or theory that claims to be above the ordinary or local accounts of social life.[18] Postmodernist social theorists argue for a return to the local narrative, and they reject the grand theory of a privileged position. In the "come, follow me" stage of discipleship, anyone is welcome to tell their story (local), but these are only viewed as perspectival. Furthermore, any totalizing story or claim is seen as being a violation of postmodern etiquette. Thus, postmodernists often reject the universal claim of Christianity because it exclusively claims to be true, not because it has been examined to be false. Therefore, the discipler must realize that potential disciples need to develop a relationship. It is through this relationship that the disciple engages the claims of Christian faith. Ultimately, when the discipler reaches the "come, follow me" stage, they must help the postmodernist nonbeliever internalize one of the foundational concepts of Christianity: God has spoken.[19] For the seeker to become a disciple, he or she must move from the inclusive "come, follow me" stage to the rejection stage of all those who would consider discipleship a shallow and naïve commitment. At this point, the discipler should stress the level of commitment that Christian discipleship requires.

---

17. Ibid.
18. Drislane, *Online Dictionary of the Social Science*. Online: http://bitbucket.icaap.org/dict.pl.
19. Shields, "Delight and Dangers of Navigating Postmodern Currents," 2. Online: http://www.next-wave.org/mar01/shields2.htm.

THE LAST DISCIPLE

REDEVELOPING RELATIONAL MINISTRIES AND LEADERS

Our churches must become communities again. It is the only way to disciple the citizens of our postmodern culture. Becoming a community requires that a church redevelop its relational ministries. It is an effort that requires strong leadership. This is, without doubt, one the most difficult challenges facing contemporary pastors.

The demands of "relational mission" are great. They are not easily quantified or measured. They are beyond mere material resources. Even so, in practical terms the challenges of redeveloping relational ministries are budgetary.

Typically, church funding gravitates toward where it will be lucrative in the future. It's called a good investment strategy. This strategy typically reinforces a cycle of spending money to make money. Indeed, a sound investment strategy ascribes monetary value to buildings, funds, resources, and even programs. By contrast, relational ministry is difficult to justify because the indicators and variables for authentic community are difficult to quantify, qualify, and empirically measure. Thus, today's churches naturally gravitate away from authentic community because it cannot be quantified or measured. Show me your church budget, and I will show you the gods that you bow to.

Strong leaders should recognize that they must create a culture of authentic community. To do so, they need to exercise vision, resources, and money toward relationality. To this end, here are some suggestions from a group of seminary students[20]

1. Look for ways to validate ministries that offer escape from the confinement of the church premise.
2. Evaluate and reduce programs with a solely inward focus.
3. Move your church beyond inadequate training by reducing the stigma of professional leadership and developing ministry

---

20. Gibbs, Evangelizing Nominal Christians, Lecture Summer 2005.

schools that are hands-on. When we fail to train our people, we set them up to be a casualty on the spiritual battlefield. Be assured, *this is a war.*

4. Illustrate for your church that the congregation is not a club, but an amalgamation of teams. As one professor of church growth put it, "The Lord owns cattle on a thousand hills, but we keep milking the same few."[21]

5. Show the difference between programmatic and need-based understanding of ministry. One example is potty training in the church. A doctoral student in Fuller Seminary's Doctor of Ministry program asked John Wimber what was the biblical justification for potty training. Wimber's reply, "Train up a child in the way they should go."[22]

6. Have classes on how to get out of debt.

7. Offer support during life transitions.

8. Question, often, if the staff are specialists in equipping the saints for ministry or running programs.

9. Finally, consider if the church specialists further their contact with the unchurched, or cut them off, because their schedules do not allow them to befriend the unconverted. Overworked staff members are always ineffective because they are not living life.

10. Strong leaders must also redefine what membership means to their local community.

This last point is so important that we need to investigate it in greater detail. There should be many opportunities for church attendees to become church members. Membership should have a functional format so that it is not granted on the basis of class completion. Rather, membership becomes, in some ways, recognition that the particular person edifies the other believers in the

21. Ibid.
22. Ibid.

local church. In this way, the office of membership becomes an appointment for a person who is already edifying the body. This model also streamlines the voting consistency by putting it in the hands of those actually working to build the local body. In this way, voting is directly correlated with those intimately involved, rather than by those who wish to influence the direction of the local body without having a real commitment to it. This also informs the voting quorum because each person can explain how a potential decision may affect their ministry. This model of membership encourages and stimulates a less difficult decision process. If only 20 percent of the people are doing 80 percent of the work, it should only be fair that these 20 percent occupy positions of decision making. Yes, I know this totally violates our democratic culture. Oh, well! As a pastor, my desire is not to create a larger voting constituency and make decisions more difficult; rather, my desire is to stimulate the saints to actively pursue the witness of Christ in their world.

TEACHING THE ORIGINS OF SCRIPTURE

The process of canonization and its touchy nephew, textual criticism, need to be a part of the church's educational process. It would be dubious to communicate such difficult and technical information from a pulpit, or even in a large classroom setting. Moreover, some communities are just not ready or willing to receive such teaching. This is an area that requires sensitivity and care. Nonetheless, many of our would-be disciples are misinformed or uneducated about how the Scriptures, in their current form, have been passed down. This would not be a concern, except for the continual attempt of the fringe groups to cut down the strength of biblical authority. While those of us who study commentaries can slip by these cajoling wranglers unscathed, most come away with scars of uncertainty. Too many scars leave these people with doubt in the Scriptures.

Challenges

So, let's put the New Testament canonization process to rest. The process of canonization—or selection of which books became Scripture—took many centuries and stages. Manuscripts were written as a record of a familiar oral story or teaching, or as an original document. Local communities chose these manuscripts based on their application, circulation, and participation in religious circles. The criteria for compiling an epistle into a collection or canon were based on the epistle's close connection to Jesus as a primary witness, (i.e., the gospels, or as a potentially original document or autograph, such as one of Paul's letters.

Now, to modern ears, the term *oral* is scary because it sounds like no one kept great records. But the first- and second-century culture proved to be incredible at remembering oral traditions. They would repeat the story enough so as not to miss even a word. For about a century and a half, until the gospels were effectively distributed, the life of Jesus was told orally, without written Scriptures. The word of God spread through word of mouth. Let us not forget that most people were illiterate, anyway.

Over time, it became evident to many people which stories were helpful for living the life of a disciple of Jesus and experiencing God as told through the Old Testament. After all, the first Christians were Jews, and their church was the synagogue. As Christianity spread to the Gentiles, the need for written Scriptures became greater as the threat of heresy increased. It all came to a head with an attempt by Marcion, who compiled the first canon of the New Testament, creating his own version of the Scriptures.

The first record of the term "New Testament" in print comes from the church father Tertullian, who, in and around the second century, used the terms *novum testamenum* (New Testament) and *vetus testamentum* (Old Testament). This usage was to combat the heretical teachings of Marcion, who attempted to subvert the God of the Old Testament as a rival to Jesus Christ. Tertullian effectively showed the continuity between the Old and New Testaments.

Then, in 367 AD, the church father Athanasius of Alexandria wrote an Easter letter to some of the churches he had been communicating with about a list of works that should be read in church. He listed some twenty-seven books in his 39th Festal Letter. While Athanasius's letter marks the first time the complete canon of the New Testament appears in print, his listing reflects a consensus that the church had arrived at much earlier—probably orally. Although debated at times, many Protestants today point to the Athanasius letter as a milestone moment in the canonization process.

Nearly all of today's translations of the English Bible have come from the Masoretic Text or the Greek New Testament. Most people (believers and nonbelievers) do not know that scholars take the scriptural variants and compile them into an eclectic version based upon the reliability of sources. Most texts of the Bible have no variation, meaning it is the most-preserved document in human history. Still, some verses have variant readings. This means that two or more codices differ in word order, words themselves, or absence of words. In many cases, variations can be simply a typographical error by a scribe writing from another copy.

The goal of textual criticism (a bad phrase for a great goal), is to get to the oldest, closest, and most original text of what the apostles or authors wrote. This is called a "critical text." If, as we believe, the original autographs are perfect, then textual criticism is a valuable venture. The Nestle-Aland Greek New Testament is perhaps the most comprehensive and trusted source for translations. It is a compilation of the best codices, whether Uncials, minuscules, or papyri. In addition, it lists in the footnotes nearly all of the other possibilities. These include Codex Vaticanus and Codex Sinaiticus manuscripts, which are considered to be some of the most reliable.

How do translators and scholars determine which codex is the most closely tied to the original? Following are some samples from a set of rules determined by Westcott and Hort, two highly influential English scholars from the late 1800s. Please note that

Challenges

these samples are listed in the order of importance. For example, the oldest reading rule is more important than the rule about writer's style. All of the citations come from Epp and Fee's, *Studies in the Theory and Method of New Testament Textual Criticism.*[23] The notes in parentheses are principles taken from sections of Hort's Introduction.

1. Older readings, manuscripts, or groups are to be preferred (§2.59, cf. §§2.5-6, 31). ("The shorter the interval between the time of the autograph and the end of the period of transmission in question the stronger the presumption that earlier date implies greater purity of text.")

2. Readings are approved or rejected by reason of the quality, and not the number, of their supporting witnesses (§2.44). ("No available presumptions whatever as to text can be obtained from number alone, that is, from number not as yet interpreted by descent.")

3. A reading combining two simple, alternative readings is later than the two readings comprising the conflation; and manuscripts rarely or never supporting conflate reading are text antecedent to mixture and are of special value (§§2.49-50).

4. The reading is to be preferred that makes the best sense, that is, that best conforms to the grammar and is most congruous with the purport of the rest of the sentence and of the larger context (§2.20).

5. The reading is to be preferred that best conforms to the usual style of the author and to that author's material in other passages (§2.20).

6. The reading is to be preferred that most fitly explains the existence of the others (§§2.22-23).

---

23. Epp and Fee, *Studies in the Theory and Method of New Testament Textual Criticism*, 157-58.

7. The reading is less likely to be original that combines the appearance of an improvement in the sense, with the absence of its reality; the scribal alteration will have an apparent excellence, while the original will have the highest real excellence (§§2.27, 29).

Finally, if one desired to study how the group of scholars came to a conclusion of one variant over another, a great resource would be *A Textual Commentary on the Greek New Testament* by Bruce Metzger.[24] In it, Metzger discusses why the committee came to a conclusion on one variation over another. Each variant is given a grade (A, B, C, D) by the scholars, based on its certainty. In this sense, it is remarkable how much the grade sways the English translation.

Regarding our English bible, it's worth noting that the church doctrine of preservation has kept the King James Bible in use for three hundred and fifty years. If you have wondered how verse designations were chosen in our English Bibles, consider the legendary story of King James who, while riding his horse, would tell scribes where to place the verse designations. It makes sense when you consider how long and short some of our verses are! Now really chapters were created by Stephen Langton in 1551 and Robert Estienne later added verse designations. Verse designation is, after all, simply a tool used for finding one's place in the text.

At this point, you get the idea. Our scriptures are God's word, but we should be shrewd in our understanding of how we receive them. Some have said ignorance is bliss. Indeed, many people are jarred when their bliss is altered. However, when one wrestles with and understands the canonization process, strength in faith emerges. The faith that this struggle builds comes from a newfound belief in the authority of the Scriptures that, in turn, can be debated in any setting. Truly, we have the most analyzed, investigated, and scrutinized communication in the history of man. It is clear that God's hand is behind it all. The fact that Jesus himself

---

24. Metzer, *Textual Commentary on the Greek New Testament*, 1–16.

never penned words of Scripture, at least as far as we know, shows God's irony at work.

God is always more mysterious and paradoxical than our imagination can fathom. In church, we often tend to sanitize the process of these mysteries. God is so secure in his Godself that he chose to pass something so sacred as the Scriptures through human hands. God did not literally drop the Scriptures down from the heavens. Rather, God created our situation just the way he wants it. He wants us to believe the Scriptures are inspired by faith.

ELIMINATING CULTURAL IRRELEVANCE

Cultural irrelevance can take many forms. One does not eliminate cultural irrelevance by simply adding new "stuff" to a ministry. Many have tried to add everything from new technologies to new programs, and much ink has been spilled on this issue; yet, the result is failure. Our churches remain culturally irrelevant. The elimination of cultural irrelevance is, in truth, not brought about by new technologies. It is not accomplished by adding or subtracting programs. It is brought about when local church leaders and local congregations change the way they think.

It is often the subtle change, not the drastic one, that produces positive effect. The elimination of cultural irrelevancy begins not with grand proclamations but with the simple act of conversation. Leaders and membership should intentionally think through each conversation they have. More precisely, they should consider the everyday words they use, and then seek to eliminate certain verbal cues that are so Christianized as to be potentially incoherent to a nonbelieving person. Simply changing everyday word use—the way you communicate—is a great way to begin changing the way your community thinks about your church. Communication style equates to relevancy. This change is more important than any minor changes churches do to be more relevant.

THE LAST DISCIPLE

Certain verbal cues in some of our churches reinforce a tight-knit community. The result, however, is slow numerical and spiritual growth. In many American churches, one can easily pick up these verbal cues. They are readily available. Perhaps the most infamous is the "brother" and "sister" cue. At one time the cue, "Brother White" and "Sister Smith" served as terms of endearment. Today these terms are Christian titles that are a pejorative in our larger society. Allow me to explain.

The infant church was inaccurately accused by the greater pagan society of incest and infanticide: Incest because of the incessant use of "brother" and "sister" between persons within the church, and infanticide because of a misunderstanding of the partaking of the Eucharist. Here's the difference: Early church models were much more socially based, in that community members shared a much tighter relational and financial network. They were a family. In a highly-charged society of socio-economic, racial, and ethnic diversity, this type of familial terminology just does not mean what it once meant. Let me put it this way: Don't call someone your brother unless you mean to integrate him as a family member. If you don't really mean it, then don't say it. In this regard, we must be careful about these deceptive cultural cues that can create more alienation than encourage inclusiveness. Churches that try to maintain the façade that their congregation is a family when they are not are, reinforce exclusion. Rather than reinforcing what is not true, our churches must be intentional. And, in order to be intentional, a church must have a serious "DTR" talk. Allow me to explain.

While we were still dating, my wife and I had, on a number of occasions, the DTR or "define the relationship" talk—a common practice of couples who are serious about pursuing a future together. In effect, the DTR was an ongoing conversation where we outlined what might happen in the future. It ranged many topics that included where we currently were, if we wanted to maintain a holding pattern of time and investment, if we needed space, or if

Challenges

we wanted to dive deeper into the relationship. This practice was helpful for clearly indicating expectations, intentions, and hopes. The DTR was also important because it made us be clear about what we were not and what we could not be at any particular point. It was a process by which we, as a couple, gauged our priorities of education, personal development, and emotional readiness. Building a good relationship is hard work, and the DTR allowed us to understand that becoming a couple required personal sacrifices that, in turn, allowed us to enter into a meaningful relationship with each other. The result of this hard work, I'm happy to report, is a healthy couple.

Effective communication in a church is like that of a healthy family; it is always truthful. These churches don't shy away from the DTR talk. Even if it is not in the interest of the church, the truth is always in interest of a relationship, and that, coupled with the elimination of unnecessary verbal cues, creates an environment that fosters cultural relevance. Churches that do this effectively attract people. They become relevant because they are refreshingly candid about who they are, who they want to be, and the type of community they want to become.

THE LOSS OF SELFLESSNESS IN THE CHURCH

As he looked up, Jesus saw the rich putting their gifts into the temple treasury. He also saw a poor widow put in two very small copper coins. "I tell you the truth," he said, "this poor widow has put in more than all the others. All these people gave their gifts out of their wealth; but she out of her poverty put in all she had to live on."

LUKE 21:1–4 (NIV)

Imagine what it was like living in Jerusalem as a woman during the first century? Let's imagine together: Perhaps in Jerusalem there lived a woman. She had grown up in a Jewish family connected to the tribe of Reuben. She used to hear the stories about the provision of God from her mother, who had told her about the way God had brought them back from the black land they called Egypt. Her mother told her about the oppressors and the emperor of Egypt, Pharaoh Ramses.

This girl became a woman and had a family. She married a fellow Israelite named Hezron; they never had a lot. He was thirteen years older than she, so that she seemed like a mere girl in the beginning. Hezron was a merchant, and, like his father before him, he sold leather to whoever wanted it. He specialized in sandals. As the Roman Empire moved in, the demand for sandals became much higher because of the constantly marching army. As a result, they prospered and were able to purchase a small dwelling on the outskirts of the city.

They had three kids together: Reuben, Leah, and Simeon (who Hezron often complained was more Greek than Jewish). Time passed, and the children grew older. Reuben had a family of his own, far away in Zebulan, by the sea. Leah died early, and Hezron and his wife mourned her death. Finally, Simeon joined the Roman army and traveled to various parts of the world. He would write, but the letters became less frequent and finally stopped coming altogether. Regardless, Hezron's wife loved him deeply, and he loved her as much. They grew old together and loved life.

But the Roman Empire, and the resulting Pax Romana, had slowly moved in. Where once there had been one or two guards on every street corner, now there were three or four. Over the last twenty years of their life, they had seen the city of Jerusalem develop around them and their family. New shops had moved in, and with them new and larger merchant stores with a wider selection of nicer leather. Hezron didn't worry at first, saying, "My relationships with our people will make the difference." But then he had to sell their dwelling. Reuben helped, when he could, but had little with which to help.

Challenges

Hezron and his wife moved into a tent. The tent had enough room for them and the thousands of sandals that Hezron would make. During the cold winter months, Herzon would wail with coughing. The final winter of his life, Hezron promised his lovely wife that he'd made enough sandals for her to sell and live out her days in comfort. Then, like the wind through the corridor of the city can blow without notice, Hezron passed on. They buried his body at a rough place outside the city. Hezron's wife kept his own pair of sandals as tokens of their love. The life he had lived on earth was one of walking, running, jumping, playing, and dancing with his wife under the Jerusalem sky. The woman hung Hezron's sandals on the pole of their tent along with the others. And she went on. She sold the sandals everyday. It only took the sale of three or four pairs for her to meet her daily living expenses.

A loyal daughter of Israel, she would visit the temple often to pray during the hour of prayer. As the years went by, the people began to call her *widow*. By the fifth year after the passing of her husband, Hezron, the woman had become quite good at selling the sandals, but she was never able to make them. Hezron had never taught her. With time, the stack of sandals diminished. Her pile shrank and, with it, the ability to provide for herself. She cut out as much as she could, no longer buying oil for the lamp for heat or light. She stopped buying meat to have with the grain. She looked at Hezron's sandals hanging on the pole of the tent and said, "Never! No, I will not sell my husband's sandals." And she wept.

Months went by and, with them, the final pairs of sandals were sold. She hadn't sold a pair for a couple days, and she also hadn't had anything to eat in two days. She felt desperate. The woman looked at that last pair of sandals. They were Hezron's, worn with years of use. She could imagine them on his strong legs, could see him walking through the streets, holding the hands of their three kids. They wouldn't fetch much, as they were well-used, but it would be something. All night the widow wrestled with selling her husband's sandals, but the hunger in her stomach provided the most compelling argument. Thus the decision was made; this last pair of sandals would be sold.

In the morning, the widow untied the strands of leather that had held Hezron's reddish sandals. For years they had dangled as a symbol of her husband's love and affection. As she pulled the string and the sandals fell into her hands, the memory of their love filled her mind. His love to her was not greater than his love to Yahweh. The sand from the Jerusalem streets was still stuck in the thin padding on the bottom of the sole, his footprint well-seated in the padding. The sandals had Hezron's smell. The leather arched over the top of the sandal and into the other side. The decoration was still beautiful. The widow took them into her hands and opened the flap of their tent.

As was her custom, the widow would first make her way to the marketplace and then to the temple. She went to a group of army stores to quickly sell Hezron's sandals. She showed them to the man at the counter.

He snatched then from her frail hands and said, "I give you one coin for them, but only copper."

She begged him, "Please, sir, these were my husband's sandals. Surely you could give more as a demonstration of your respect for the dead."

"What do you think this is, *charity*?"

She persisted.

He said, "Fine. Three copper coins. Now get out of here!"

The widow imagined how she would spend this final money. Perhaps she'd treat herself to a great banquet meal with her friends, or buy a large amount of grain. Maybe she would purchase a room in a hotel so that she could remember what nice linen felt like. She weighed her options. As the time of prayer approached, she had yet to spend her money, and she went on to the temple.

Before she went inside, she saw a blind man begging at the temple gate. She said to herself, "Well surely I can spare one coin." She gave it without her left hand knowing and went inside.

Challenges

The rabbi that day spoke of the many needs of the city and was so compelling with his plea that he won the hearts and minds of his listeners. The widow was also touched. She thought of all the needs this rabbi had mentioned and considered them to be greater than her own. As a matter of fact, her needs seemed to slip away. Perhaps if this rabbi had known the widow's state, he would have insisted she not give, or perhaps he would even have given her the offering. After the rich had given, the widow went to the coffer and she put in the two small copper coins—it was all she had.

The Modern Challenge

The lesson of the widow's offering is not really about the amount that one gives, but the relationship one has to God and to community. True relationship with God transforms a person's attitude toward life as one of giving ourselves away. I could share some modern stories of individuals who also gave sacrificially. There are the grandmothers who live on social security checks week-to-week and give what precious little is left. They are the college students who are faithful despite circumstances all around them. They are the high schoolers who work part-time jobs and give their entire income to missions. They are the retirees who are the volunteer base of the local church. And all of these people give not because of charity but because of their love of Christ. Unfortunately, this should be normal in church culture, but increasingly it's becoming the exception. I suspect this has something to do with the way we have made church culture more comfortable over the years.

There is an ugly underlying reality when we make church too comfortable. Church becomes about us. In such a comfortable church—even a wonderfully well-intentioned church that attempts to create a user-friendly environment—rather than seeing the commitment we have to our neighbors and the people in our community, we can lose sight of this element of the gospel. While I believe that church should be user-friendly, this usability can come at the high cost of low commitment. In such a situation, the focus of the church is on receiving rather than giving. In such a church, members feel entitled to service from God rather than feeling commitment to serving God and spreading the good news. Recall the widow's story: At no time does she focus her desires on receiving.

Truly you must strike a balance in your approach to making church user friendly, but not at the cost of selfishness. We need to rediscover what it means to give ourselves away. That of course begins with the leader. Now, our church history is rich with lessons to help us avoid selfishness. Allow me to demonstrate how quickly the pendulum of church culture can swing from selflessness to selfishness, and what happens.

After our Lord was born, died, and resurrected under the Roman government, the church of Christ was persecuted. The Book of Acts shows and indicates the way in which this persecution emerged and was carried out. This persecution spread from a Judaic persecution of the "Jesus people" to an empire-wide persecution, because the Gentiles were now experiencing the regeneration of the church. The first major obstacle that the church faced was Gnosticism, ultimately culminating in Marcion's canon and his ideas about the new nature of God. The response of the church was the eventual development of the Christian canon. The gates of hell did not prevail.

Amid the end of the first century and into the second, the church experienced a greater challenge in extended and intensified persecution. Tertullen, a church father, said, "The blood of the martyrs is the seed of the church." Although, in the beginning, the pockets of persecution provided a galvanizing growth for the infant church, empire-wide persecution under Diocletian was extremely damaging. This time period was so dark that the church was almost snuffed out. This is where many of the stories of early martyrdoms come. The tide was turning, but it brought with it a new challenge—the combination of a church-state. This began

Challenges

with the emperor Constantine, who became open to Christianity after the battle of the Milvian Bridge.

In 313 AD, Constantine, as he was baptized when nearing death, abolished and forbade the use of crucifixion as a method of capital punishment. There is something significant and profound to be said of a government that was involved in the death of God and persecuted his followers. But these thoughts and sentiments are even more profound when applied to a government that reverses itself in thought and deed. Christians began holding positions of great influence in the Roman Empire. This empire had become rich with gold. The wealthy church leaders began to change the instruments of death. Wooden crosses became golden crosses. These were the same church leaders who had readily identified with Christ's statement that "No servant is above than his master, if they persecuted me, they will persecute you," because they had suffered loss of status, limb and, for some, even life. Thus, a generation of Christians who still had the scars from their persecution under Diocletian began to forget. Yes, they remembered the words, but where to appropriate them? They now wore their golden crosses as symbols of wealth, status, and power, rather than carry their wooden crosses of self-sacrifice to places of surrender.

As it was in the second century, so it is becoming today. Church leaders need to constantly take personal inventory to ensure that they are not abusing their positions to pad their personal well-being. This is not an easy task. Our larger culture is focused on the gratification of the self, so much so that the very systems and structures of society have become consumer oriented. Leadership must be vigilant in making sure that church processes aren't focused on just generating a clientele and turning out products that make people feel more comfortable. We must not create consumers who like Christian products. We must create disciples who are sacrificial in their lifestyles. That is, we need to develop people who understand the mission of the gospel is one of self-sacrifice through development of the spiritual practices.

Church leaders have choices. Following the Christian consumerist path leads congregations to the wastelands of spiritual and cultural irrelevance. But following the path of Christ allows leadership to rediscover much needed spiritual practices that can be imparted to our people. As Christ teaches, one way to blunt selfishness is through prayer. Due to the gravitas of this challenge, we will address the issue of prayer again in the next chapter.

EMBRACING CHANGE AND ITS CHALLENGES

Our society and our culture of church have undergone significance changes. They continue to change, and we must change with them. We must especially change in how we undertake discipleship in an urban and postmodern context. We can be in a position to adequately address the changes in our time if we retool the discipleship models and create more relationally centered ministries.

We cannot continue the attempt of discipleship through mass production. The shifts in population, the church's role in public life, and the changes that urbanization have brought to the average American family require a diversified approach to doing ministry. Urbanization has also created groups with distinctly different needs. These groups cannot be ministered to out of a box. One size does not fit all. There is also a desperate desire for authentic community that mass-production ministry cannot fulfill. This is why churches must move beyond simply having church services.

We must reexamine and discover new ecclesiological tools for making disciples out of converts. We haven't fully realized the extent to which our abandonment of discipleship has cost us. In the overuse of evangelism techniques we have tended to foster a weakened state of discipleship. The invitation to a spiritual journey is a good start to a discipleship model of our time.

Postmodernity presents challenges and opportunities for the invitation to discipleship. In one sense, postmodernity is a return to a supernaturalist worldview in that it coalesces belief around emotions and relationships rather than on rationality. It follows that if relationships and emotions are the locus of belief, then community naturally becomes a critical component in a modern ministry model. But a church community does not exist in isolation. Due to the large amount of misinformation that circulates in our information-oriented society, it is necessary for local churches to teach the true origin of scripture. Churches that openly and honestly confront these challenges will experience a transformation from cultural irrelevance to societal consequence.

5

Best Practices

EVERY LOCAL church should strive in its ministry. A striving church tackles the challenges posed in the previous chapter. As well, a striving church keeps its theological and practical framework simple enough that it can build from them.

There are six best practices that a local church must undertake. They are effective communication, great compassion, dependable community, selflessness through simplicity, refreshing authenticity, and intercessory living. Notice that there are several common elements of ecclesiology within these six areas. These common areas include teaching, preaching (evangelism), compassion for justice, community, selflessness, simplicity, discipleship, authenticity, and prayer.

Striving church leaders will engage in these areas in order to develop a more realized ecclesiology model through a more empowered community of believers. Each individual in the kingdom is given a gift. These are mutual, dependent, and diverse gifts. The role of clergy, then, is redefined into that of a facilitator. I believe this is a more accurate representation of New Testament missiology. These practices can help to foster an environment for greater demonstration of ministry.

EFFECTIVE COMMUNICATION

Effective communication is a primary goal of the Pentecostal Church. Bringing a kerygmatic word has been an essential part of growing the people of God. If the church's mission is to prepare and proclaim a theological event based on the Word, which is the method of preaching in most ecclesiologies, then this event must become a daily movement. It should not be consigned merely to a formalized practice on a holy day. Of course, preaching is not only something that happens among believers. (This idea seems to be a fallacy of the modern church.) Preaching happens whenever a believer proclaims the gospel as public truth[1] to unbelievers in any public setting. Indeed the proclamation of the gospel takes many forms of communication. But communication becomes preaching when it is practiced in the context of unbelievers, whether that be in the marketplace, college campus, the public park, the high school or wherever. This idea is articulated by C. H. Dodd at the end of his study on the difference between preaching and teaching in the New Testament. After an exhaustive study that included every reference to preaching and teaching, Dodd concluded that preaching was a theological proclamation to unbelievers, and that teaching was theological proclamation to the people of God. Thus, it is my opinion that, in order for the church to attain true ecclesiality, a kerygmatic proclamation is an essential ministry. Let me say this in another way: a local assembly must create space for the public proclamation of the gospel.

Fellowship in the context of teaching is an equally important aspect of effective communication. Fellowship is an event that validates the truth of teaching. However, the implications of fellowship are still within the bounded set of interpretation where Scripture has the place of primacy. The affirmation of gathering around truth is important because it reemphasizes the fact that truth is embodied. This truth is not simply something that is arrived at axiomatically in Greek syllogistic thinking. This type of philosophical logic does little, if anything, to help the seeker of truth to ascertain truth, itself. The truth is embodied in the person of Christ, himself. Again a theological mystery, the imperative for

---

1. Here I refer to Leslie Newbigin's *The Gospel as Public Truth and Proper Confidence*.

Christians is to locate truth in Jesus. This imperative also allows us to bypass some of the issues that arise in the postmodern mindset. For example, if we want to know the truth about losing our friends, we look at Jesus, who, when he loses his friend Lazarus, doesn't draw up an answer to theodicy about why bad things happen to good people. Rather, Jesus weeps. There is, in the expression of his humanity, what all of us need to know when we cannot find intellectual answers to explain reality.

GREAT COMPASSION

My grandfather John and his family grew up in Germany during the Second World War. They were a middle class family, but because of the war they had to move to slum-like apartment complexes with many Germans. They were starving, and many families from the apartment complex would go to the field by the apartments and pick the farmer's corn for food. My grandfather and his brothers and sisters wanted to go pick too, but his father, my great-grandfather, told them not to do such evil. "God will provide. He will give us justice."

During this time, my grandfather went to look for a job to get food. He went to a factory owned by the Nazis and began to speak to the guard about work. He tried several different languages, but to no avail—until he tried Bulgarian. My grandfather found that they needed help in the kitchen, and he had some experience as a chef. He worked many hours that first day making food for this despicable army that would cause destruction for years to come.

After his shift, my grandfather grabbed his coat and began to pick up all the leftovers. He began putting them in his coat, and the head chef stopped him and said, "No, John. Those aren't for you. These are for you." He filled my grandfather's coat with fresh fruit and vegetables, and with meats and cheeses.

My grandfather wept. He did not expect this, especially from these people. After all, my grandfather hadn't asked for any of this.

He brought the food home to the apartment he shared with his family.

As he brought the food to his father, his father said, "Call the neighbors; let us show them the faithfulness of the Lord." My grandfather told me several of the people in that apartment complex came to faith, and some of their families are still serving the Lord, today. The lesson that this story teaches is simple. When we understand that God's provision for us in difficult circumstances is for the blessing of society, there will be biblical justice.

A lack of biblical social justice is one of the most common criticisms of the Pentecostal mission. It is a somewhat valid critique. Advocates of a Pentecostal approach to mission believe that our focus represents an "other world" religion.[2] What has happened, according to advocates, is that in the early years of Pentecostalism we were so focused on the end that we neglected social issues. However, a closer look into what transpired reveals that this is not necessarily the case. I would argue that Pentecostalism was both a cause and effect of social change. Even though Pentecostals have not written much on the treatment of the poor, it was because, primarily (especially in the early years), Pentecostal Churches were churches of the poor. Furthermore, although evangelization was the focus of the mission for Pentecostals, it was not at the exclusion of social concern.[3] Within this model, a major mission's paradigm is God's love, and the poor as social outcasts are the subject of that mission.

Pentecostals have created their own alternative institutions that function as methods of human justice. In addition, Pentecostals question why others haven't seen that there are other alternatives, aside from political, to improve society. Political methods have their place, but as a singular model they create gross inefficiencies and corruption. Effective social change takes place at the communal and micro-structural level, not just at the macro-structural level. In this, Pentecostals and Catholics agree that com-

2. Kärkkäinen, *Toward a Pneumatological Theology*, 179.
3. Ibid., 183.

passion ministry is essential in mission, and that the kingdom of God is the ultimate expression of social justice. When persons come to faith they are saved not by good works but unto good works. If we live in the Spirit, then we must believe that we can do good works like no one else can. Although we have demonstrated compassion to our members we must also be in cooperation with other agencies in our communities. The church can be an agency of social change by proxy through regeneration of its members. Change of society must be both inward–out and outward–in. We must hold social ecology and the individual spiritual experience together in tension.

Nonetheless, it is paramount to establish a documented theology of social justice. While doing this, the Pentecostal movement will need to maintain its focus on evangelism and reengage social concern, knowing that these are met in conjunction with people who have been changed by the Spirit. Those changed by the Spirit can be integrated into their communities and affect change on the micro-level.

DEPENDABLE COMMUNITY

> *Trust in the Lord with all your heart, And lean not on your own understanding; In all your ways acknowledge Him, And He shall direct your paths.*
>
> PROVERBS 3:5, 6 (KJV)

Trust is one of the most necessary practices of any institution. It lubricates the processes of any organization. It is the essential building block of social capital. When trust is eliminated, red tape and bureaucracy take over. Societies themselves thrive or die on the basis of trust. Indeed, trust is the basic principle of any social contract. When a flight suddenly becomes turbulent, an experienced pilot will alert nervous fliers to "Sit tight and stay seated." They are basically saying, "Trust me. I see what's ahead."

At the local church level, when we model trust we create dependable communities. We create a culture that has a God-dependant attitude that says, "God, we know you have our very best in mind." Church leaders who model trust and follow through with trustworthy leadership help to foster a trusting environment. Trusting one another is crucial for community to develop among the members of a church. Trust decentralizes the roles of church members and allows a greater number of people to minister. If a person knows that you trust them to follow through with a task, and that person knows you are counting on him or her, then that individual is motivated to complete the task. Trust eliminates the need to micromanage. Do you need to verify? Sure, but there is little need to have a triple-check system. Trust allows more people to produce. Having a loyal and dependable culture means that no one needs to manage results. Instead, church members manage relationships. When trustworthy relationships become a reality, the results are dependable.

When there is a lack of trust, church teams typically mask their weaknesses and hide from constructive feedback for fear of reprisal. And when a team breaks down completely, a third party is sometimes called in to assess the problems and prescribe remedies. This type of triangulation does not belong in the church. Church teams that follow the principles that Jesus laid out in chapter 18 of Matthew solves so many problems. People who are members of cultures of trust admit mistakes and apologize for shortcomings on a regular basis. This sort of honesty is also fantastic for creating positive attitudes.

How do you begin to cultivate trust in a church team? You begin by modeling openness and consistency. You demonstrate that you have the best interest of others in mind. Your team will follow this lead. Your predictability is an accurate gauge of the future behavior of your church team. Don't rush the process. Time creates cohesion. Churches that cry, pray, and play together, stay together.

THE LAST DISCIPLE

SELFLESSNESS THROUGH SIMPLICITY

> *My house will be called a house of prayer, but you are making it "a den of robbers."*
>
> MATTHEW 21:13(NIV)

Jesus often quoted Isaiah, especially when communicating about the kingdom culture.

> *These I will bring to my holy mountain and give them joy in my house of prayer. Their burnt offerings and sacrifices will be accepted on my altar; for my house will be called a house of prayer for all nations.*
>
> ISAIAH 56:7 (NIV)

Jesus chides groups at the temple to fend off the systematic attempt to capitalize on people seeking access to God. Jesus hones in on their selfishness. The fact that we are God's temple is important, in that prayer is a place to fight the vacuous attempt by our culture to refocus attention on ourselves. As the author of Acts notes, "God is not housed in temples made by human hands."[4]

As was noted in the previous chapter, one of the challenges facing our churches is the loss of selflessness. Selflessness is a foundational virtue of our faith that can be lost through a high-paced lifestyle. Likewise, selflessness can be gained through living simply and allowing the rediscovery of the spiritual life of Christ to satisfy your soul. We are reminded that the journey of the spiritual life begins, first, with one foundational component: God speaks. This is the foundation of our faith. It requires listening. It requires prayer. God speaks in a variety of ways, but we must begin with this foundation. To begin the authentic life, it is not simply enough to pray a prayer to God. We are changed when we come to know

---

4. Acts 7:48, NIV.

that not only is there a God to whom we can pray but one from whom we hear.

Among evangelicals, a pandemic of one-sided perception and communication with God has occurred. A constant verbal prayer life betrays an egocentric problem. Many people have come to me and said, "Dave, I can't hear from God." What I tell them is this: "Quiet your mind. You are sitting under the Master. While he graciously receives your petitions, he already knows what you need, before you even ask it."

What makes more sense in a Creator–creation relationship: more input from humanity or more input from divinity? The spiritual journey is one of listening and seeing, rather than of speaking and being seen. Recentered on Christ, one who conducts a Christocentric prayer life receives a vital well. It is full of deep water that quenches thirst when received with a quieted mind. Christocentric prayer begins with trust. Trust that the time is valuable. Trust that you do not have to bring some capital, even input, to the table. Trust that the words of Christ are regenerating, even in their subtle admonishment and encouragement. Trust in knowing that his affirmation is not predicated on your performance but on his faithfulness to you. Out of grace, his intercession toward you, through both his words and presence, is sanctific (in the sense that his words and presence are continuous). Saturation is essential for hearing. Christocentric prayer is one of the most difficult to loyally, faithfully assume; but it will reap a harvest of integrity, solidarity, and vitality to those who practice it.

So, we begin with God speaking. Once one has established listening to his ministry through the time spent in Christocentric prayer, the journey assumes the warp and woof pattern of reciprocation.

THE LAST DISCIPLE

REFRESHING AUTHENTICITY

We desperately need to find our humanity. Our humanity is really just the interaction of love to one another in its purest form. When we see a reflection of ourselves in the other person, we begin to experience empathy. Empathy comes when we have character and integrity in ourselves. All of these elements come together as the result of the rediscovery of community. People in great communities, especially communities of faith, understand that this happens in its truest form when we embrace truth with both hands.

Becoming people of truth requires love. We are never simply called to take on those who propagate false information in the world. Jesus didn't simply call the Pharisees on the carpet for adding to the law. Rather, Jesus—in love—pointed out their misrepresentation while he simultaneously embodied the truth, so that it was clearly seen. A Pharisee named Nicodemus responded because he saw the truth in love embodied.

We can't point out falsehood without embodying truth. It simply isn't effective evangelism. Paul said, "Follow me as I follow Christ."[5] Because Jesus was the embodiment of truth, we are called to be the same. Truth is not purely a validity and actuality established in the mind, but rather a consummation of mind and heart. People must seek the truth from a good teacher, one whose life is a demonstration of truth through love. A.W. Tozer said, "Thirsty hearts are those whose longings have been wakened by the touch of God within them."[6] As written in Eph 4:15–16: "Instead, speaking the truth in love . . . the whole body is joined and held together by every supporting ligament which grows and builds itself up in love as each part does its work."

We who have a measure of truth are required to be a being of truth through loving those who do not have the truth of love. This is not apologetic or philosophical. Through no human argument

---

5. 1 Cor 11:1, NIV.
6. Tozer, *Pursuit of God*, 22.

can a family find love. The Scriptures teach us that our former way of life is to put off your old self, which is deceived by its desires, and be made new in our attitudes and minds. The passage, Eph 4:25, says, "Therefore each of you must put off falsehood and speak truthfully to his neighbor, for we are all members of one body." Being a person of truth requires that you see yourself the way God sees you. When we fail to do this, we lose touch with our very self. We detach ourselves from our heart and begin to live a double life. Fredrich Buechner expresses it this way, "Our original shimmering self gets buried so deep we hardly live out of it at all . . . rather, we learn to live out of all the other selves which we are constantly putting on and taking off like coats and hats against the world's weather."[7]

To become a person of truth, it is not enough to know what Jesus taught or even to admire his teachings. Until you have assumed his teaching into your consciousness to the degree that you act on them, you do not understand the spiritual. In a very real sense that which is practical and applicable to life, Christ asked his followers to lead. Once you embody the truth, you will find your humanity.

INTERCESSORY LIVING

Churches with a systematic and regular practice of prayer tend to grow. They grow numerically, but more importantly, they grow spiritually. While an individual's spiritual growth is unseen (except to God), fervent, systematic prayer is what distinguishes an institutional church and a kingdom-growing church. A church without prayer can grow, but it does not grow the kingdom of God. The reign of God can only take place where God's people have a relationship with him. The best have found ways of integrating their relationship with the Lord into every aspect of their life. They are listening and hanging on to every word he gives them.

Our prayer should be touching heaven with the needs of earth. Life in God is just one long conversation with God. Our

7. Buechner, *Telling Secrets*, 45.

intercessory lifestyle is a quilt of conversations with the people we love. Our Father has a way of weaving all of the little squares together with a divine stitch that, if we listen and follow his words, creates a global tapestry of love. We must be global intercessors with a global intercession, because the kingdom is global. Prayer is not an option for consideration; it is an assumption of Jesus. In the gospels, teaching on prayer constantly begins with the words of Jesus, "And when you pray."

Prayer helps prepare people to build integrity and develop character. When we pray, we are hearing God open our hearts to unseen things. If this is a regular practice, we discover that God, who searches the untraceable, knows the very secrets of our heart. *Listening prayer* opens a door to character development in a way that Scripture reading alone cannot do. If we undertake a systematic study of the Scriptures, we build a foundation for God to communicate the nature of seeing "kingdom come" in our heart. In listening prayer, God uses those biblical principles to teach us specific applications for our circumstances. There are gray areas in some of the decisions that we, as believers, will face. Only God knows the ultimate outcome of those decisions, and, moreover, he knows our intent for making decisions in the way that we do. It is certainly possible to do the right things at the right time but with the wrong intentions, and in so doing absolutely lose what would have benefited the kingdom. Prayer is the equalizer for the ego, the sanitizer for the libido, and the galvanizer for the spiritual.

As good as a Pentecostal ecclesiology is, it's nothing if not lived out. The preceding practices reaffirm the relationship between charisms and the church as an institution in a local context. It is incumbent upon the leader to gauge whether the outcomes of each practice are sufficiently addressed or if more vision is needed to focus upon them. The key is a participatory ecclesiology where leaders serve as exemplars and as facilitators. The church is a spirit created and sustained; and yet it is a human institution. Creating space for each of these areas empowers believers and encourages them toward greater participation.

Part 2

Christology:
Thinking Like Jesus About the Church

The second portion of this book looks at the theology of Jesus (including Isaiah's role in the life of Jesus), his eschatology, his most important sermon topic (the kingdom of God), and the implications for humans being made in God's image.

As a result of the fall, the church cannot always embody the kingdom of God. But when the church does embody the kingdom, the salvific work of Christ occurs. When this happens, the power of redemption creates a nexus for discipleship. That is, a community begins to see that its highest cultural pinnacle is the embodied truth in the person of Jesus.

When a community sees that this highest ideal is not just as an idea on a page, but is a life to be lived, the process of discipleship begins. An individual in such a community does not enroll in a program to become a disciple. Rather, discipleship is a condition in which an individual takes up the teachings of Jesus and follows them to their ends. No program can create such a condition in an individual. But the right spiritual guide can motivate each of us to become the disciple that Christ has called us to be.

PART 2

Christology:
The Living Jesus About the Church

6

The Incarnational Nature of God

In the beginning was the Word, and the Word was with God, and the Word was God.

JOHN 1:1 (NIV)

The Word became flesh and made his dwelling among us. We have seen his glory, the glory of the One and Only, who came from the Father full of grace and truth.

JOHN 1:14 (NIV)

What does "he ascended" mean except that he also descended to the lower, earthly regions? He who descended is the very one who ascended higher than all the heavens, in order to fill the whole universe.

EPHESIANS 4:9–10 (NIV)

CHRIST'S WORK AND THE IMPLICATIONS

CHRISTOLOGY BEGINS with a theology of the cross and ends in soteriology. Of all the major religions of the world, Christianity is the only one that is represented by a symbol of death. The lotus, the six-pointed star, and even the crescent moon are elements of future and light. But the cross is the symbol of defeat, death, and destruction. This extreme symbolic gesture is the representation of how regeneration comes from the life and death cycle. This informs every aspect of our teachings and theological basis for preaching. It is, nonetheless, unintelligible to those who do not believe.

If the martyrs, and their blood, are the seeds of the church[1], then Christ's salvific work on the cross represents the ultimate act from which this blood flows. Christ's death on the cross is like a seed, deep in an ancient forest of giant sequoias. The seed is held within a hand-sized cone that can lie in wait on the forest floor for more than sixty years. If a wildfire approaches, it is a fire that will destroy everything in its path. All life and hope will be lost to defeat and death. But, paradoxically, the fire that destroys everything else is necessary to the sequoia seed. The fire's intense heat releases this one seed from the dormant cone. And in this way, life takes root. Like the dormant sequoia seed, Christ's death creates the nexus for life. The purpose of the sequoia seed is to wait for the fire to release its life. It is this life and death cycle to which we must draw the attention of humanity. The cross is the center of christological proclamation because in Christ's death we, paradoxically, see life.

In regard to the humanity of Christ, we say that Christ descended. We do not say that he ascends. To do so would be to have an upside-down Christology. Christ is not a man who somehow gets it right, nor is he a man who lives a perfect life and in so doing becomes God. Rather, Christ is true God, from God—*begotten* not *made*. These phrases are from the Nicene Creed, and they distinguish the Christian church from sects such as Mormonism. The Nicene Creed implies a divine kenosis, or divine emptying. In one sense, Christ becomes what only God could become as humanity—a servant. Servanthood is the true nature of God, no matter what form God chooses. The trait of servanthood distinguishes our God from other straw-man gods. Worldview and theological constructions that feature a god coming to humanity through a

---

1. A saying of the early church father Tertullian that historically has been part of early and late Christian theology.

show of force illustrate a profound misunderstanding of God's true nature. In turn, adherents to these views demonstrate shallowness in the discipleship of Christ.

As we look in chapter 2 of Philippians, we see the nature of the church clashing with the nature of Christ. If the nature of God is humility, given his supremacy, it begs that we, as the church, see humility as one of the ultimate aspirations of our community. The unification of the body of Christ occurs when its members practice humility. Paul writes that if we feel encouragement in the compassion, comfort, and fellowship of Christ, then we should not seek more feel-good virtues; rather we should seek humility.[2]

Humility is one of the rare virtues that can be manipulated. However, there are virtues that cannot be manipulated. For example, there is no such thing as a false patience. You are either patient or you are not. A false compassion is not possible. One has it, or one doesn't. But one can have false humility. Jesus talks about this practice of the pious. Many church folk fall into this trap. It is a natural result of fallen nature. False humility fouls the Lord's name with the filth of its lie. However, a church that is representative of God is a church that does not exhibit the classical pharisaical pitfall of false humility. Such a church is a place of ultimate service and authenticity.

The verses Phil 2:6–8 relate an early hymn of the infant church. Here, Paul includes a discussion of Christ's humility. He writes that Christ volitionally takes the nature that is in the truest sense of his Godself—service in humility. Again, it is a paradox that, in his Godhood, Christ can be omnipotent and, simultaneously, a servant. Thus, he incarnationalizes. In this manner, he becomes an agent of healing. The church father Gregory of Nazianzus writes of God's incarnation, "That which has not been assumed has not been healed,"[3] as a way to indicate the virtual necessity of Christ to be fully human—to experience the full gamut of humanity's

---

2. Phil 2:1, NIV.
3. Sollier, "Apollinarianism." *Catholic Encyclopedia*, 14.

range—and in so doing becomes fully man. This dichotomy of dirt and divinity leads us to several ramifications.

First, the extremity of the cure implies the severity of our disease. We have to learn the lessons of what we have done. That God is driven to the point of incarnation seems to indicate that all other options had been exhausted. His previous attempts were all foiled by humanity's failure. This failure begins with Adam and Eve's sin, and then continues with the failure of the patriarchs, Noah, and the people of Israel. Throughout the biblical narrative, there is an underlying theme: God constantly has to start over because the wickedness of humanity constantly breaks his covenant. After Adam's sin, it takes three chapters of the Bible for God to begin anew. God tells Noah that humanity is so depraved he is literally going to start over with Noah. Later, God makes a covenant with Abraham, but Abraham fails to hold up his end and commits adultery with his wife's servant. And again, after God brings Israel out of Egypt, he is disappointed with his chosen people because of the idol they have made—even while he is giving Moses the law. In Exod 32:9, God tells Moses that he is going to destroy his chosen people and start over with Moses. If it were not for Moses pleading with God, God would again have started over. The lesson is clear. Our works result in failure. Our depravity is a sealed fate. What we have become as fallen humanity is so destructive that, even when we attempt to live at peace, we do violence to ourselves and our own humanity. Indeed, we endure the ramifications of these human failings with the polarization of the Western and Middle Eastern worlds. Like a constant graffiti, we deface on a daily basis the image of God that is written in our DNA, without thought or consequence. Without the intervention of Christ, we would be reprobate.

Second, we can assume some realities about our humanity in the eschaton by looking at Christ. This first reality is seen in the bodily resurrection of Christ, a distinction that again reinforces the uniqueness of Christ's work. Note the physicality of his bodily resurrection. He still bears the holes of the nails in his hands, the

The Incarnational Nature of God

gash in his side, and at times his appearance is recognizable. Paul makes it very clear that our bodies are part of the spiritual whole. Even in our physicality we are constantly eternalizing ourselves. This is why piety is vital. Otherwise, let us eat, drink, and be crazy because we are going to die. In several places, the Bible indicates a level of permanence to our bodies. Popular religion tends to caricaturize spiritual bodies and the unimportance of here and now. Such gnosticism is very much alive and well. The words of Jesus and Paul tell us that nothing is arbitrary. *Everything matters.* Everything has consequences. How we treat our earthly bodies is reflected in our heavenly bodies. Again, the example of Christ leads us: There are lasting consequences to our actions and to the actions done to us, such as the nails driven through the hands of Christ. The biblical account notes that, after Christ is resurrected, Thomas sees the holes in his hands and even touches them.[4]

What about people whose bodies are damaged, or who experience the loss of limbs in a war—how are we to understand these physical realities in a spiritual body? Indeed, what are we to make of the paradox of Jesus' resurrection body with his healing work provided in the atonement? No doubt, there is a tension here. This is a tough conversation to have with your uncle who has no legs to stand on because of life-destroying cancer. I'm not saying that we will not have a metaphysical wholeness to our resurrection bodies—to be sure, a resurrected body is a healed body. I believe in supernatural healing. But I do so in context of the whole of Scripture.

When we take the whole of Scripture—if we take it seriously—we see that even the effects of sin may not be without eternal consequence to those who are saved. Please understand: Christ's work destroys sin. But the effects of sin, whether positive or negative, will still be felt. A couple of examples seem appropriate. First, this effect can be seen in the violation of a rape in which a child is produced. In this instance, the consequences

---

4. John 20:24–29, NIV.

of a terrible mix of lust and violence produce an eternal being. A child made in the image of God. This one act changes both the nature of physical and spiritual reality. A second example is the act of a murderer who kills a person who has not received salvation. This unsaved murder victim goes to hell. In both cases, Christ's work forgives and can redeem both rapist and murderer by destroying sin, but the physical effect of their sins ripple in eternity. Again, this one act changes both the nature of physical and spiritual reality.

What we do with our physical bodies is not arbitrary. The God who made us spiritual beings has given us physicality, which is also part of our metaphysical wholeness in eternity. Thus, we can see the importance of not being a glutton or a masochist. Lest we feel hopelessly trapped by these examples, we are thus refocused upon the death of a physical Christ to redeem our corrupted bodies.

There are many today who reject this notion, arguing for a metaphysical dualism. They separate soul and body; still others separate soul, spirit, and body. (Watchmen Nee is a classical example of a person who ascribed to such dichotomies.) While some of these distinctions are semantic, there is nonetheless some scriptural grounding for them. It seems that you almost have to be a dualist to be a Christian; but perhaps not. The point is that Christianity is different from other religions in that we believe in a bodily resurrection that calls us to holy living because we understand the nature of resurrection.

This truth raises an important question: What does it mean to be created in the image of God? We can arrive at some inferences by looking at Christ as an archetype. This is a topic that I explore in the next chapter.

7

The Image of God

He is the image of the invisible God, the firstborn over all creation. For by him all things were created: things in heaven and on earth, visible and invisible, whether thrones or powers or rulers or authorities; all things were created by him and for him. He is before all things, and in him all things are held together. And he is the head of the body, the church; the beginning and the firstborn from among the dead, so that in everything he might have the supremacy. For God was pleased to have all his fullness dwell in him and through him to reconcile to himself all things, whether things on earth or things in heaven, by making peace through his blood, shed on the cross.

Once you were alienated from God and were enemies in your own minds because of your evil behavior. But now he has reconciled you by Christ's physical body through death to present you holy in his sight, without blemish and free from accusation—if you continue in your faith, established and firm, not moved from the hope held out in the gospel.

COLOSSIANS 1:15–23 (NIV)

THIS PASSAGE links us with Christ as an archetype of humanity. It also draws the lines of distinction between *created* and *Creator*. This passage also reveals that Christ is the fullness of the Godhead, bodily. He is the image of the Godhead; Father, Son, and Spirit in flesh. This passage is the major foundation block for the Chalcedonian formula, which has been used as a mark of orthodoxy for more than fifteen hundred years. Christ, as son, does not represent a punctual change in the makeup of the Trinity, for it is a decision God makes within the Godself. We say that Christ is "eternally begotten of the Father." A paradox to the doctrinal construct of God's immutability is that the incarnation happens in a point in world history. Thus, we must hold God's immutability in that he providentially chose Christ to appear during the first century Judaism. The early church quickly moved beyond the details of Jesus' earthly lifestyle to embrace the ontological reality of Jesus as God. This move is reflected in the creedal confessions of the Church. Although these creeds are necessary, they are not sufficient. When our understanding of Jesus as God is reduced to a creedal statement such as in the Nicene Creed, "light from light, true God from true God, begotten not made," we lose the dynamic of Jesus as a real man—eating, drinking, and teaching.

When we look at God in the form of Jesus, we see a human. An essential part of Jesus the man was his ethnicity—his Jewishness. Jews, as some have said, are some of the most religious people in the world and, when secular, are secular like it was their invention. God, even by his very action, says, "I will be your God, and you will be my people." They are his people, because he is one of them. We see God as a child, as a boy. He learns a language and then another. He is, at some point, realizing he is God. Can you imagine God in puberty? And yet, through him, even as frail as humanity can be, are all things created. That God creates ex nihilo (out of nothing) is incredible in itself; that out of Jesus all things have their being through the life and resurrection of Jesus deepens our understanding of the life and death cycle. Before there is a new creation, there first must be a creation. Out of atoning death comes life that reaches back into eternity and paves the way for the Spirit to brood over the dark waters and bring light. Perhaps we can see in Jesus the light of the world through the lens of earthly creation. The One who is our spiritual light is also the One who gives physical light. Moreover, that God was pleased to locate the fullness of his deity in Christ provides a strong case for the desire

The Image of God

of Almighty to dwell among us. He desires that we participate with the Sacred, even on the base physical level. It is the spirit of Christ within each of us that gives us the capacity for discipleship and mission. Divinity desires participation with humanity. It is always his desire, first, not ours. Obviously, we have a choice to participate in the divine. Indeed, the will of the Spirit allows us this choice. And so it is our own arrogance and hubris that separates humanity from its maker. And so we must embrace Christ's work of atonement on the cross.

Humanity is created in the image of God (imago Dei in Latin) and, therefore, has inherent value beyond utility or function. This image is not predicated on our relationship to Christ. Rather, it is the effect of God's creation of humanity. However, when our relationship to Christ is established and the image is consciously realized, the creative process of God is actualized through his creation. This can be seen in decision making and rational processes such as deliberation and self-reflection. Given our freedom to be like God, we are also able to act in free will.

Acting in freedom can result in fallen activity. Humans can, and often do, decide to oppress their likeness to God. But humans can also express the ultimate understanding of this likeness through acts of love for ones' neighbor. Love becomes the realization that the other is, in effect, a representation of God. Thus, when Jesus quotes the two greatest commandments, he is teaching us to love God through God's love and through loving those created in his image.

The image of God that we see in ourselves is multifaceted. We see in the biblical narrative that God created us both male and female. There are elements of God we can assume are both male attributes and female attributes. There are elements of creation that are derived from God, which we can assume come from God's personal nature. Thus, the compassion and tenderness that come from a woman's touch are as much a part of God as are masculine might and strength. So we see the divine artist at work. Look at the wheat fields, the hues in the skies, and the innate details of the tree, all working together in a symphony of sights, sounds, tastes, and feelings. Then, we come back to the ultimate creature of God's creation, which is humanity.

EMOTIONS AS PART OF THE IMAGO DEI

Jesus was the fullness of the Godhead, bodily. He was God, and he had emotions. He was human. In John, we see Jesus weeping over the dead body of his friend Lazarus.[1] We see him weep, and we can say, "Look, my God has emotions." This is just one passage, of many, that has implications for developing a theology of emotion. Scripture is full of emotion coming from both God and man. While some scholars might denote God's emotions as anthropomorphic, the incarnation mitigates against this. That is, Jesus' response to Lazarus's death is one of many examples of emotion in response to God's activity or his inactivity, for whatever reason, in the world. As leaders we should also have a emotional response to the dark side of the fallen world, such as in the case involving Lazarus. Thus when we see or hear of violent acts that do not cause us to have the feelings that we should, we need to evaluate our response. We need to wonder why we are not feeling emotions. Could it be that we've desensitized ourselves? Could it be that we have not aligned our intake with the will of God so that the emotional outtake—the response—is a negative one? Whether or not you see it, God's emotionality informs our emotional approach, not just theoretically but in some applied ways. While this work is not the place to explore all of the psychological concepts that are informed by an imago Dei anthropology, I would like to briefly explore a couple emotions. Certainly, we can see this emotion in Jesus. This is one truth, when studying the life of Jesus, we can readily pursue. This pursuit of emotion is not a show of theatrics. This pursuit is a means for embracing empathy, an emotional response to another.

1. John 11:35, NIV.

The Image of God

Jesus was empathetic to the humanity around him. In the Gospels, he sees that the people were "harassed and helpless, like sheep without a Shepherd."[2] Let's not forget that he wept over Jerusalem.[3] These are different examples of his passion. This passion is not sympathy. Jesus moves beyond that. Jesus does not gloss over what moves him, and then forget. As followers of Jesus, when we are confronted with an event or act that troubles us, we must honestly respond.

Unfortunately, some churches respond to the troubles of others with lip service. We can also be extraordinarily aggressive in some of our sermons in pursuit of the pure emotion. These services are hypercharged, over-spiritualized roller coaster rides. Conversely, we make services so dry, so emotionally irrelevant, that people separate their emotions from their relationship with God. In both cases, whatever true feelings that might exit are drawn out and then robbed of their meaning. People come away drained, tired, and desensitized.

Jesus has emotion that was empathy. This empathy is compassion. He was compelled to action. He moved beyond sympathy, or even feelings of guilt, to a compassionate response that activated others. He moved toward a solution. Certainly, we see that Jesus did not respond to every single person as they wanted him to respond. He was not a door mat for the world. But he moved beyond the simple expectations, the sociological pecking order, and the common cultural mores of his day. He moved beyond race and gender to meet people at the point of their need. Jesus broke some of the suggested boundaries that the religious culture of that day mandated. When we are reminded of the woman at the well, or the Good Samaritan story, or Jesus being called a friend of sinners, these are accounts of the edgy nature of fringe-ministry by Christ.

2. Matt 9:36, NIV.
3. Luke 19:41, NIV.

Always there has been an attempt to pin scandal on Jesus. However, Jesus went into potentially character-damaging situations (against common wisdom) not because he was looking to create controversy, but because he was moved by a person's need. He did so because of his empathy. And we cannot detach Jesus from his empathy. To truly follow Christ's example in this area, we may at times need to "break social rules." Empathy is a critical emotion for fulfilling the many aspects of Jesus' primary message in the Sermon on the Mount. We cannot authentically laugh with those who laugh, or mourn with those who mourn, until we empathize. We must care. And to the extent in which we care reveals the extent of the image of God in our humanness.

The emotion of anger, when it is a righteous anger, is a residual aspect of the image of God. Jesus exhibited anger when confronting the outrages in the religious arenas of his day. Jesus could not abide the dangerous and sinful acts committed in the name of God, in the place of God, and he was swift to confront them. We must also resolve avoiding super-tolerance. Negative things will be said about us.

If we are followers of Jesus, we too should be angry at the hypocritical and Pharisaical spirit that pervades some of our church culture. Righteous anger should culminate in a response, such as in conflict. Conflict is not bad. Conflict is a necessary component of our Christian faith so that we can come to a resolution.

Jesus also had great courage. We can debate whether courage is an emotion or not, but there must be an emotional response for courage to actualize. Obviously, at the end of the day, courage is simply taking action while being afraid. The courageous individual goes boldly forward while feeling a mixture of fear and uncertainty. This mixture of emotion and action is called "courage." We can see acts of courage in many modern examples, such as Rosa Park's stand against racism. She sat down. The rest is history.

Jesus confronted the different problems he faced with courage. This emotion—this fortitude—can often be mistaken in peo-

The Image of God

ple who are stoic. But Jesus was no stoic. Jesus is a metaphysical composite of all emotions. We, as believers, don't want to overspiritualize this, but surely we could say that, if Jesus is the Son of God, and if he is God incarnate, and he is a genius, and if we believe he is the answer for humanity's problems, then we have to come to a place where we accept that Jesus emphasized and exhibited some genuine emotions that we need to emulate. Nothing is more relevant to this emulation than courage.

In this sense, Jesus embodies the essence of justice. Justice isn't an emotion, of course. You could say, however, that justice is related to mercy. We see mercy in Jesus. A just society requires merciful people. A society that is a place of vengeance is not a just society. In addition, a just society mitigates escalation. (You did this thing to me, so then when I retaliate against you, I will up the ante.) Indeed, Jesus deemphasizes escalation and emphasizes forgiveness. Followers of Jesus must be merciful, for mercy is a prerequisite to forgiveness and de-escalation.

A great example of de-escalation is the Cold War. The Soviets told the Americans that they would de-escalate the situation by removing a weapon, so that, in good faith, the Americans would pull back one of theirs. This created a positive reverse cycle. American presidents from Gerald Ford to George W. Bush have quoted Just War theory concepts before the United States declared war.[4] They do so in order to delineate and meet certain criteria as reasons for war, and thus assume the role of a just country whose hand is forced into war. (Both the Geneva Convention and Just War theory is based on Jesus' understanding and concepts in chapter 18 of Matthew and the Sermon on the Mount.)

The brand of justice that Jesus teaches is remarkably relevant to our everyday lives. Life is not fair. There are things that are not going to be fair in a place where God has allowed a level of freedom to take place. Nonetheless, God, in his wisdom, finds ways of allowing mercy to take place. In a world where forgiveness is not

4. Stassen, Kingdom Ethics, 160–80.

in focus, we can expect people to want to retaliate. This is a natural outcome of our fallen nature. It takes the Savior to remind us of the true power of forgiveness.

We all have personal conflicts in our day-to-day lives. Even the best among us are accused of minor misdeeds. We are not perfect. Then again, none of our accusers are perfect, either. When confronted with such accusations, regardless of who is in the right, we should say, "I'm sorry," or "I apologize." We can say this on behalf of ourselves or the organization we represent. Or we could say this on behalf of our accuser. Nonetheless, it is amazing how much wind is taken out of the sails of an argument or disagreement because it appears as though we are not interested on conflict. This simple act of mercy begins the de-escalation process. Rational discussion can then follow.

Then there is love. Jesus was the Savior of the world, but he saves us one person at a time. Salvation is not a mass production experience. This salvation is genuinely authentic. Jesus understands that salvation takes genuine relationships, built and cultivated on kindness through time. He shows us these qualities in the time he spends with his disciples. Jesus built relationships in a way that show us the personal nature of God's love. Had Jesus created a large group of disciples—say, one hundred or even a thousand strong—then his demonstration of personal salvation would be muddled, if not lost altogether. The crowds that followed Jesus existed because he healed their diseases. He had a charismatic draw because he met their individual needs. But these crowds did not exist because of his love. However, at the end of the day, the twelve disciples followed him and modeled him as a result of the love he showed to each of them. He showed them a deep love they'd never before experienced in their lives. This love, culminating on the cross, was exhibited in Jesus' toleration of their stupidity, acceptance of their frailty, and acknowledgement of their humanity. With full knowledge that they would screw up from time to time, he loved them nonetheless.

The Image of God

PHYSICAL MAKEUP AS PART OF THE IMAGO DEI

God's image is represented in our physical bodies. Certainly we can relate our physicality back to God as creative artist. The large scope of his brush renders each human absolutely unique and significantly different. And, because he's done this, our physicality reaffirms his magnitude and the great span of his image. Our differences are based on a million details and wrinkles that God has spun around each individual. The effects of time, space, and geography each play a major role in the more significant aspects of an individual, such as coloring of the epidermis, body size, and the manner and amount of outward decoration. It is very rare for individuals to share an accumulation of such traits—even between twins. It is a unique and amazing aspect of God's imprint on our humanity. Each potential human birth represents a continually growing aspect of God's creative imagination. How is it that each face looks different; each hair strain is singular in its own way; each bone structure is uniquely fitted? Could we say then that God's imprint on humanity—his image—attests to his continual growth as creative Creator, given each new child's uniqueness? Even still God is not physical. The Scriptures do not communicate anything regarding the physicality of God's deity. Nonetheless, the spiritual God and our physical nature are enmeshed.

You have to wonder how God looked in Jesus. Jesus was not extremely beautiful, visually stunning, or stately. The only biblical description we have (if we interpret it to be about Jesus) demonstrates that Jesus was somewhat plain.[5] Early historical descriptions of the Christian God suggested plainness. But later, the emphasis changed.[6] What does that say about God? Perhaps a better question, what does that say about us? Looking for the answers about the relative physical nature of Jesus the man reveals our own shallowness about our physical nature, does it not?

---

5. Isa 53:2–3, NIV.
6. Latourette, History of Christianity, Vol. I, 44.

THE LAST DISCIPLE

Let's think about this in the context of Jesus as he is depicted within culture. If you have ever stopped to look at the divergent faces of Jesus throughout different cultures and eras, you have no doubt noticed that Jesus looks like "us." In a Caucasian culture, Jesus is depicted as Caucasian. In an African culture, Jesus is depicted as African. In an Asian culture, Jesus is depicted as Asian. This should be no surprise. Humans have to relate to God through our own physicality, down to our very culture. It is interesting that we have not gotten beyond this way of representing Jesus. Perhaps we never will. It is equally interesting that we put a face on a Supreme Being that demands no such tribute from us. Perhaps there is no other way for us to come to terms with such an awesome God. It suffices to say that we have to be careful that we do not worship those images.

When you close your eyes, how does Jesus look to you? If you are a typical American, the chances are he looks like the iconic American fair-haired Jesus—despite the fact you know Jesus comes to us from a Jewish culture in a Middle Eastern community. It is an indication of how strongly cultural powers can influence the working out of one's spirituality.

SOCIETY AS PART OF THE IMAGO DEI

God is Creator in community. He exists within a social network of the Trinity. Moreover, Jesus was birthed in the context of a community and within a family. God did not simply decide to have an adult Jesus come down and appear in a flash of lightning. God is not interested in cutting corners socially. After all, God created the very concept of family and community; and community is the means by which God creates human society. Jesus comes to us, socially, from the bottom-up, not from the top-down. This is to say, God was reared as a child. God, as Jesus, developed within a human community. As this notion relates to our communities and churches, it is critical that we recognize the image of God as

The Image of God

he shines through our children as they develop from one stage to the next.

This is not an anomaly from God's typical pattern. To date, childhood conversion is the largest mode by which the church has made disciples. Scripture is not silent in this regard. All of the Old Testament covenants (Adamic, Noahic, Abrahamic, Mosaic, Davidic) are predicated upon the assumption that they will be fulfilled through children. The Shema, which is central to Judaism, commands that children be taught who God is.[7] The Old Testament laws, the psalms, the gospels, and the epistles of Paul all have prescriptions on raising godly children. The major themes include teaching them discipline, the law, and about God. Statistics demonstrate that children come to faith when they grow up in a Christian home where there are two parents who are active spiritually.

Raising godly children requires active families and good communities. Good families make even better churches. Paul, the apostle, spends some time talking with Timothy in this regard. One of the qualifications Paul gives to Timothy is that the church leader's family should be in good order. Why? The leader's family ultimately becomes the blueprint that the local church will use to raise their children.[8] There is a real correlation between a breakdown in the family and the presence of dysfunction in society at-large. This correlation also exists in the local church. The Scriptures are replete with examples of dysfunctional families, from the patriarchs to the household of David. Without a doubt, the fragmentary nature of church movements is connected to our fallen nature, which is also expressed in the family unit.

God is able to work through dysfunctional families, of course. But a unified family is his original design for the nurturing of children. A unified family has a number of essential elements in operation within the home. These elements are community,

7. Deut 6:4–9, NIV.
8. 1 Tim 3:2–5, NIV.

education, worship, and service. Children need to learn how to become active members of faith, and an active faith-based community provides the context for practicing the other essential elements. As such, a unified family in the form of a father and mother provides the foundation for such a community. Because each parent brings unique traits to the family, each can demonstrate the behaviors, beliefs, and activities that constitute an active faith. This education comes about through verbal, and especially non-verbal, demonstrations of faith. Verbal education comes in the forms of devotionals, reading assignments, and bible reading. Non-verbal education is demonstrated by examples of the right types of emotions and passions. Worship takes place together, as a family, at a local church. The worship experience gives a corporate feel to the personal faith that the children experience in the intimacy of the home. Finally, service is the natural conclusion and combination of the other three elements, and is practiced in faith.

The modern society presents great challenges to these essential elements of community, education, worship, and service. Our children, our families, and our communities are all affected. Greater technological connectivity has blurred the lines of work, home, friends, cities, and family. The mobility of this connectivity instantly, literally, brings the world into the home. Without parental vigilance against this digital onslaught, the intimacy and communication of the home can easily break down. In addition, many children enter into the world beyond the family with more than just their parents' voices to guide them. These children have been influenced by the voices at Head Starts, day cares, and in-home nannies. The impact of these voices translates to lessened educational control that is prescribed throughout scripture. The blurred realities of upward mobility can also present a challenge for children, families, and communities. Upward mobility routinely separates families geographically, and for extended periods of time. The consequences of this separation, beyond the fracturing of family and community, also include reduced opportunity for family worship, which is related to education.

Make no mistake, education is the greatest biblical theme regarding children. Children need a socialization process that takes into account the comfort of intimacy and agency of human freedom. Intimacy becomes vitally important as the basic human freedoms of curiosity begin. Human freedom is necessary to explore the world. However, what keeps us all warm at night is not the affinity of an explored community, but the proximity of a loving family.

CHILDREN AS PART OF THE IMAGO DEI

The imprint of God in our children can be seen in their faith. They are naturally interested and curious about the world and, just as naturally, they have gaps in their knowledge. They faithfully trust their parents, and the people who care for them, to fill those gaps. This trust is not something that we teach them; it is something they do naturally. It comes from the imprint of God.

Children desire an "upward" relationship with adults. This is beautiful. By this I mean, children are not solely interested in having relationships with their peers. They long for, and even crave, relationships that include parental attention and affirmation. Tragically and sadly, most adults seem to encourage children to outgrow these upward relationships as quickly as possible. It is a wonder that we don't recognize this aspect in our communities. Perhaps we adults are overly interested that our children exhibit independence, to our own social and spiritual detriment. It is interesting, however, that to varying degrees adults never outgrow a need for upward relationships. Adults have mentors. Adults have coaches. Adults have teachers. That is, our need for upward relationships changes little throughout life. This need illustrates a basic human necessity. Seeking upward relationships has always been a part of the human landscape of spiritual journeying.

Let Jesus be our guide.

8

Being Born in Christ

BEING BORN again is a daily process of constant repentance. This truth is illustrated through the conversation Jesus has with Nicodemus, a Pharisee, in John 3:1–21. Jesus tells Nicodemus that, in order to know God, one must be born from above and anew, once again. The Greek word for *again/above* (*anōthen*) alludes to Jesus' emphasis of continual regeneration. This regeneration is achieved through the process of spiritual rebirth; and Jesus desires that his disciples practice unceasing repentance in order to be continually reborn in the spirit.

An open posture of the heart and the attitude are necessary for spiritual rebirth to take place. Still, attitude is not enough. The spirit of God comes to a person with an open heart and so fills the soul of one who is dead. In this way, a person becomes as first born. Jesus understood that spiritual rebirth was an integral part of his mission. It was through this rebirth that his followers believed in him. When we walk in the principles of Jesus, when we are reborn, the wind of the Spirit changes us and we see with new eyes.

Through these new eyes, the kingdom is unveiled to us. We see the sublime truth that heaven grazes the edges of the earth. We see that living life itself—even our very breath—is part of the great orchestration of the One who is its source. Through these new eyes, we see color hues become richer. We see all of our actions in high definition. We see that death is little more than a fallen leaf on the floor of a lush forest.

Born again in the spirit, we see ourselves for ourselves, for the first time. We see ourselves, because we see him. But this insight is not simply introspective. Certainly, the kingdom is within us, but we must recognize that the kingdom also resides within our neighbor. The other becomes the self. When we look into each other's eyes, it is not brazenness or shallowness we sense, but depth and meaning beyond what mortals can bear. He is in us, and we are in him. In him, we live and move, and our being becomes more than the total sum of its doing. More than ever before our action and our being coincide. We see that as we relax our posture, our will becomes entwined into his. Because his will is not frustrated, we find peace with ourselves and with God. We see, through love, the elements of the kingdom and the active places that God designates for creatures in the garden of his creative process. These places may be places of tumult and dimness, but we understand they will produce great music and fruit. Our senses—what we see, hear, taste, and so on are new. We are born again!

As we are born again, the spirit in our heart cries out Abba, Daddy! *Father.* Our Father adopts us as his sons and daughters. The theme of adoption is strong in the Scriptures, both on the physical and spiritual level. The God of Jacob sees foreigners and orphans in the land of Egypt and hears their cries. He brings them out. Adoption is strong in the narratives of Ruth and Naomi and Moses in the river. And, in a very real sense, Jesus himself was adopted by Joseph. With God's adoption, we are no longer defined by the things done by you, to you, or against you. You are no longer defined by the fact that you were abandoned by your father or that your mother was a deadbeat. Instead, when you are born again in the spirit you are able to acknowledge that you are *yourself.* You are created in the image of God and born in Christ. You are defined not by your former life, but by your adoption; and with your adoption comes promises. You are no longer defined by your past, but by the person you can become. With an adoption such as this, you become like Christ: a gift to others. You become a gift to the world. You understand that there is so much more possibility, potential, wonder, and beauty for your life. You begin to think of your life in terms of how to live a life of integrity, how to be a person of truth; and in so doing, you learn how to be more compassionate. When you are born again, you are no longer defined by your worst moments—you are defined by Christ.

COMMUNION

Communion is a tradition that our Lord passed down so that we may remember him. The meal that he shared with his disciples was the Jewish Seder, which included the bitter herbs, the tastes of honey, and the eating of the lamb. During the meal, they drank from the cup four times. This is now the church's communion. It is a tradition of the church that Jesus did not get to the final cup. He drank the first two, the cups of Sanctification[1] and Deliverance[2]. It is clear from the Scriptures that Jesus had them sing from the Psalms, as the Seder is traditionally celebrated. Then he stopped with the third cup, the cup of Redemption, and said, "This is my body." Then Jesus said that he would not drink again until all Israel is saved. The final cup, the fourth, is the cup of Consummation. Every time we remember his death through the act of communion, we anticipate the day Jesus is seated at the table with the cup of Consummation in hand. At the end of the age, we will be made complete because of his work. In this sense, the activity of the Kingdom within us is not complete; we are made in his image, yet with defect. But on that great day, we will have true union with God, without defect. This is the event in which we participate.

Imagine the Father, Son, and Spirit sitting with us as we commemorate the meal of the Lord. They invite us to participate in the divine dance of unity. When we take the cup and the bread, we should, as Augustine said, take it "with a mouth of faith." Tertullian said that the Eucharist was "the medicine of immortality." We know that is not the case, but something happens during the time

---

1. "I will take you out of Egypt."
2. "I will deliver you from Egyptian slavery."

of remembrance. Don't worry, I'll stay true to our Zwinglian doctrine, but I have seen many healed during our commemoration. How weird is it that Pentecostals believe in miracles but hold so strongly to the Lord's Supper as merely symbolic! The cup and the bread are not the Host. They are commemorative. But, if God can use a handkerchief to heal the sick, then expect God work miracles through the bread and the cup.

COMMUNION, THE CONTINUATION OF REBIRTH

When one has been born into Christ, he or she enters into community with the triune God. The corporate practice of communion is a symbolic and spiritual rite of the local community between God and man. It is also a commemoration meal of anticipation for those who are born again. First, the meal anticipates physically having the Seder meal with Christ at the coronation of his kingdom. Second, the meal is recognition of the new covenant. Each believer shares with Christ the new covenant: if we will put our faith in Jesus, then he will forgive our sins. The meal of the Seder is recognition of Jesus as both sufficient high priest and perfect sacrifice. And because of his unique duality, as both high priest and perfect sacrifice, he is able to forgive sins as we are born into him. This is more than a remembrance meal; rather it is a spiritual event in the continuation of being reborn, in which the participants, rather than the elements, are to be transformed. The implication is that we follow Jesus as into death and resurrection.

9

The Kingdom of God

Christians know that the kingdom begins with a Messiah who died between two thieves in the place of the Skull. Jesus was nailed to a cross. He was crucified. But if you are like many, you have grown numb to the reality of the cross. I do not mean reality in the sense that the cross is a religious symbol. By reality of the cross, I mean its literal meaning as a form of capital punishment.

Let us consider the cross in its actual context. Crucifixion was a common form of capital punishment, practiced throughout the Roman Empire. To the people living during the time of Christ, the cross was not a beautiful symbol. The cross was a very real instrument of officially-sanctioned torture. The cross was synonymous with agonizing death. That a self-proclaimed Messiah would willingly accept death by crucifixion was utter foolishness. And that this Messiah would be crucified at the Skull, a place outside of the city walls where only society's worst was executed, only confirmed the Pharisee's condemnations.

In truth, knowing these facts means little to us today: we do not have a meaningful context for understanding them. Perhaps it would help if I contextualized the foolishness of a Messiah crucified. Remember, Jesus was condemned to die by the religious elite of his day. It was a politically motivated execution meant to eliminate the inconvenient reality of who Jesus was. What would that look like if it happened today? It would probably look something like this.

The trial of Jesus would be televised. There would be pundits on both sides of the isle. CNN and Fox news would be live in the courtroom. Outside, a raucous crowd would wave signs. Some would say "you're condemning the innocent." Others, "He was inciting a riot." Still others would suggest that it is expedient for us to eliminate the hate mongers like Jesus from our midst. The morning talk shows would discuss this man with a Messiah complex. On-air experts would conclude that Jesus needs to be medicated because he thinks he is God. They would ask how his dedicated group of followers can take him seriously.

Do the Messiah and the kingdom begin to seem foolish to you?

Then comes the day of execution. Because the government is responsible for conducting the peoples' business, Jesus is housed on death row at a federal prison facility. It's a place of the Skull if there ever was one. This is where the filthiest of humanity are caged while they wait to die. Jesus is escorted from his cell. He walks down the aisle and looks with compassion on each person he passes. As he passes by the cells, a man with tattoos wrapped around his arms and chest is screaming. The man has stretched his hands as far as he can between the bars. "Remember me Jesus, remember me!" The guards allow Jesus to stop long enough for him to look the man in the eye and say, "Paradise is on its way."

But the guards know the truth. Paradise is a fool's errand—a pipe dream. Crazy talk.

As the guards lead the condemned into the execution chamber, an unseen weight settles on Jesus. The guards cannot figure out why this is. Jesus is a strong, blue collar man. It's like he is carrying the weight of the world on his shoulders. So, through the doorway, the guards have to lift Jesus across the threshold. A crowd has gathered in the viewing area. Jesus can see his friends and family through the plated glass. His mother puts her hand on the window and one of his best friends, John, consoles her. The glass begins to fog with the heat of the hands and the tears in the crowd. Near the back, a few watch over the gathered to make sure that the execution actually goes according to plan—that Jesus actually does die. Where is the wise man? Where is the philosopher now? Indeed, why would a Messiah so willingly allow himself to be put to death in such a way?

Remember what Paul says that to kingdom outsiders, this execution is madness.

The orange robe is ripped. Prisoner number 777 is torn. His back is bare. The handcuffs come off. Jesus sits down onto the cold, metal chair. He drops his forearms onto the arms of the chair between the stirrups. The straps go over his wrists. His hands turn red from squeeze of the straps as the guards tighten the knots. Then they secure his feet. On his head they place a crown, a bowl of metal. Even a sponge he is given. The water runs down and the electricity is flipped. It flows. It courses through heart and lungs and fingers and tongue—through his entire innocent body.

This is the King of kings and the Lord of lords. But for the moment we all seem crazy.

This is the foolishness of the cross. This is the foolishness of a kingdom based on the crucified Messiah. It is also, according to Corinthians, the power and wisdom of God. And as foolish as it seems, the cross stands as the greatest single symbol in human existence. The cross divides human history. The cross embodies personal sacrifice. The cross commands our devotion and invites us to life after death. This is the coming of the kingdom.

The cross is Abraham's faith confirmed. The cross is the end of Joseph's nightmare. The cross is Moses' serpent statue in the wilderness. The cross continues the reign of David's throne. The cross confirms the wisdom of Solomon. The cross cuts Nehemiah's cornerstone. The cross is Isaiah's prophesy fulfilled. The cross is Job's answer. The cross gives doubting Thomas certainty. The cross breaks Onesimus's chains. The cross gives Peter stone-like strength. The cross swallows sin, destroys death, and crushes the enemy. The cross brings us to the kingdom. The cross demonstrates God's love, and says do this in remembrance of me. The cross provides healing. The cross extends mercy. The cross is what makes us holy. The

The Kingdom of God

cross is what Paul preached. The cross is the Christian's destiny. The cross is what Jesus died on. But the cross was not his end. The cross was the beginning. The cross was why Jesus focused his preaching on the kingdom. The cross demands that we follow him.

The primary concern of Jesus's preaching is the kingdom of God. This is very clear from the synoptic gospel accounts. This is clearly Jesus' favorite sermon topic. From the use of similes, "the kingdom of God is like . . ." to the number of parables, Jesus always attempted to define the kingdom. He would say the kingdom is like finding a million dollars in a field, or that it is like discovering the crown jewels in the oddest place. But what did he really mean when he spoke of the kingdom?

According to Jesus, the kingdom of God is not a kingdom of boundaries. The kingdom is a condition of being in and among the people of God who are experiencing God's kingly rule. And yet, God's spirit is not windblown in a vacuum; it is within his people. Thus, when Jesus speaks to people about the kingdom, he uses words such as *enter, inherit,* and *go into.* To be part of the kingdom means that one experiences a relationship like one might have with a president, ruler, or king. And yet, God's rulership is marked by peace, mercy, redemption, and a land of new promise. As Isaiah communicates, "How beautiful on the mountains are the feet of those who bring good news, who proclaim peace, who bring good tidings, who proclaim salvation, who say to Zion, 'Your God reigns!'" (Isa 52:7).

THE KINGDOM IS AMONG YOU: LUKE 17:20-21

One cannot overemphasize the experience of the kingdom within community. In Luke 17:20-21, Jesus locates of the kingdom of God within us all. When the Pharisees asked when the kingdom of God would come, Jesus replied, 'The kingdom of God does not come with your careful observation, nor will people say, 'Here it is,' or 'There it is,' because the kingdom of God is within you."(Luke

17: 20–21*).* Commentary writers conjecture as to the exact translation of *entos humon,* or "within each person"; but, nonetheless, it is commonly concluded that Jesus is telling the Pharisees that the kingdom of God is experienced when two or more of God's people get together. Jesus is saying, in effect, that the kingdom of God is the condition that occurs when people who have the kingdom in them come together. It is that sharing of relationship, by simple proximity, with the King that creates sharing in the kingdom. Thus, in this passage, we see Jesus inviting the Pharisees to join in the kingdom.

The Kingdom Suffers Violence:
Matthew 11:12 and Luke 16:16

In Matt 11:12 and Luke 16:16, Jesus poignantly talks about the kingdom suffering violence.

> *From the days of John the Baptist until now, the kingdom of heaven has been subjected to violence, and violent people have been raiding it.*
>
> MATTHEW 11:12 (NIV)

> *The Law and the Prophets were proclaimed until John. Since that time, the good news of the kingdom of God is being preached, and everyone is forcing their way into it.*
>
> LUKE 16:16 (NIV)

Does this mean that the kingdom of God is under attack? The answer is yes and no. It would seem that Jesus was saying that "the kingdom of God is being opposed with violence." That is, people are using violent means to compel others not to be part of God. On the other hand, this is also probably an allusion to both the preaching and style of Jesus' disciples and of John the Baptist. This preaching style involved telling people of the kingdom in a

The Kingdom of God

way that required them to make a decision—the kingdom must be taken by force. The notion of force also refers to the movement of unbelievers who try to get into the kingdom of heaven without regard to the expectations of religious people. Take, for example, the case of the Jewish believers who thought that the Gentiles needed to be circumcised (even though they did not). The Gentiles were literally looking for a desperate means to force their way into a part of the kingdom. And beautifully, our loving God allows it.

The "Already/Not Yet" Nature of the Kingdom

A traditionally accepted understanding of the temporal aspect of the kingdom of God is the already/not yet theological construct. This construct posits that we are already a part of the kingdom, because of the incarnation of Jesus Christ and his influence in humanity through his work on the cross. Still, the kingdom has not yet come in its fullness due to the effect of Satan (ruler of the kingdom of the air), and his influence in the world.

There is a battle between the kingdom of darkness and the kingdom of light. Differences flourish about the give-and-take battle between these two kingdoms. But the point of the construct is that we are caught in the middle, awaiting Jesus and having not yet witnessed his return. Some have said Jesus nearly destroyed the demonic work of Satan (as can be seen in the accounts in the gospels with the exorcism of demons and the raising of the dead), and that we are simply part of the mop-up mission in the aftermath of Christ's victory. Others see the coming of Jesus as the empowerment of his disciples to the degree that we will yet do greater acts in the name of the kingdom. This debate leads to much conjecture; nonetheless, the "already" and "not yet" nature of the kingdom has been initiated by God. God initiates the kingdom with the coming of the King, and we await its consummation with the return of the King.

THE LAST DISCIPLE

When Jesus talks of this consummate moment in human history—the eschaton and his return—he always reminds us not to worry about its timing but to focus on preparedness. The consequence of preparedness, like any good Boy Scout knows, is to find out about the nature of an impending force. Preparation for the coming of the kingdom compels us to discover it.

What are kingdom characteristics? Note that the kingdom activity, in the words of Jesus, is never monolithic, either to God or humanity. The kingdom comes from both divine and human activity. This coming is not simply predicated on God's action. This is why we, as those who carry the kingdom within us, are called to seek after it. Moreover, Jesus never uses the word *built* in reference to the kingdom. Rather, he uses words such as *inherit* and *seek*. These words illicit a mutual action on the part of a humanity striving for the love of God, and, for God, out of his love, moving on us through the Holy Spirit. A great place to look, and begin to understand, the kingdom that Jesus describes is at New Testament references in Isaiah. Jesus often quotes Isaiah and the Psalms. Isaiah depicts aspects of the kingdom. See Matt 13:14, Mark 4:12, Luke 8:10, and John 12:40 for Jesus' quotes of Isaiah (Isa 6:9–10) about people not understanding parables. In Matt 15:7–9 Jesus quotes Isaiah (Isa 29:13) regarding the religious elite. In Matt 21:13 and Mark 11:17, Jesus quotes Isaiah (Isa 56:7) regarding the temple as a house of prayer for the nations. In Mark 9:44 Jesus describes those not entering the kingdom and hell by alluding to Isaiah (Isa 66:24). In Luke 4:18–19 Jesus quotes Isaiah (Isa 61:1–2) about preaching in the kingdom. In John 6:45 Jesus quotes Isaiah (Isa 54:13), demonstrating that he is the subject of the teaching. In addition to Jesus quoting Isaiah, the gospel writers use Isaiah passages as biblical descriptors of Jesus as the Messiah. For an example, see Matt 1:23 for the quote of Isa 7:4 about the Messiah being born of a virgin.

The Kingdom of God

The Kingdom and Culture

The kingdom is, of course, not a place but a state of being. It's a condition. The Old Testament hope for salvation is not simply a transcendental, a spiritual, and an eternal hope. It is also a physical and bodily hope that is freed from captivity and exile in a foreign land. The kingdom is where God's will is done on earth as it is in heaven.

There are various interpretations of the role of the kingdom in our culture. Two great questions can guide us as we endeavor to make the kingdom a greater influence in our society today: To what extent should the people of God participate in the greater society? How should the people of God perceive Jesus and his relationship to culture?

Helpful at this point is Richard Niebuhr's *Christ and Culture*[1]. In his work, Niebuhr gives a history of Christian responses to the world's culture. There are five major points:

1. Christ against culture
2. Christ of culture
3. Christ above culture
4. Christ and culture in paradox
5. Christ the transformer of culture

"Christ against culture," according to Niebuhr, is the interpretation of those who are viewed exclusively through a Christian lens of history as being the rise against pagan society. There is a tendency in this camp to withdraw from greater society. Ultimately, Niebuhr sees this as inadequate.[2] As noted in chapter 2, the local community forms its interpretation of the gospel by both the reality and perceptions of the local church. In my opinion, this creates

---

1. Niebuhr, *Christ and Culture*, 11–45.
2. Ibid., 65.

theological voids (see chapter 3) for both the local community as well as those in a local assembly.

"Christ of culture" is an interpretation of history as being the interaction of the Spirit and nature. One of the great aspects of this position is that Christ has a universal appeal of the gospel. The statement that Jesus is the savior of the world, and not just for our little group, is more logical. In this view, Christ and culture have an equal authority. Christ becomes culture's highest achievement. Yet there is a tendency here to view culture uncritically. This is manifested today in certain arms of church culture, and in varied ways. While one group may baptize a worldly culture, another group may have a difficult time seeing the value of Christ if there is little difference between him and what culture has to offer.

"Christ above culture" is the view of history as being preparatory under law, the age of reason, and the story of the gospel. It consummates in the union of the soul and God. This view, as well as the other two that follow, has a greater recognition of the complexity of the enduring Christ-culture problem. There is recognition that Christ enters into the realm of the world not at odds with it. Rather, Christ comes into a world that is godless. In this view, the benefits of culture come only through the grace of God. And the grace of God can only be understood in context of cultural activity in the world. In my opinion, this is a reasonable position but seems to work better in cultures that already have a large Christian influence, because it tends to speak more to the culture of Christians than the Christianization of a culture. The logic of this position breaks down with cultures that have had a rise and then decline of Christianity in their society. I am also concerned that this position can, at times, reduce the ministry of the charismata in culture due to the elevation of Christ above it.

"Christ and culture in paradox" is an interpretation of history as being a struggle between unbelief and faith. This view recognizes the truly radical nature of the gospel according to Jesus, and that the gospel claims cannot easily assimilate into culture. In modern America this is the most common view. This position affirms the irreconcilable nature of the kingdom of light and kingdom of darkness. It creates a truly civic religion, and that is problematic because of the duality that it creates. The duality limits both the realities of God and culture to spheres of life. As a result, you have faith being relegated to a private life and not in the public sphere. I think this position has been the most damaging in church history. Consider that this position produced the concepts of the sacred and the secular in Luther's theology of two realms. The duality of the sacred and the secular is fundamentally flawed because it doesn't account for the reality of all of creation being from God. This is especially true in its view of the division of man between the spiritual and the physical. Note my view on metaphysical wholeness in chapter 6. This position is also less helpful for ministry to a postmodern generation that neither separates spheres of life nor the spiritual from the physical.

"Christ transforming culture" is the view of history through the eyes of a conversionist. It is a hopeful look toward the future that redeems a perverted culture and returns it to its original designs. For Niebuhr, this last view represents a real-time renewal of the soul, versus a focus on what will happen in the end, or what happened in the beginning. This view seems to have a soft take of sin. Moreover, its categories for the transformation of culture are abstract and seem to come off sounding like the western concept of progress. Still, the transformation of culture is revolutionary, and one could certainly say that of Jesus.

Each of these categories are a relevant and continued part of church culture toward the different cultures in which it finds itself. All cultures have traits that affirm and disaffirm the likeness of Christ and his kingdom. This includes church culture. Syncretism aside, understanding how to better contextualize our churches in the American mission field will improve the ideal of the kingdom coming. Many baptize the culture and send it to the pew or create such a small microculture in their church that unbelievers cannot relate. Looking constantly for ways to affirm aspects of culture that are Christlike helps create transformational models that allow people to begin to see Christ through modern eyes. When this happens, they see the kingdom of God for the first time.

The kingdom of God begins with the foolishness of a Messiah who died through means of capital punishment on a cross. Yet Jesus' invitation is not simply to join him in death; it is also an invitation to live life the way he did, and in a similarly radical condition. When people seek and go after such a condition, marked by the peace, mercy, and redemption of God's kingly rule, the kingdom of God comes into their lives and the lives of those in their influence. This kingdom is within each believer and is more fully experienced when two or more individuals come together. The kingdom of God advances in spite of the violence against it, and people are desperately forcing their way into it because of the life it brings. This type of life in the kingdom that Jesus describes comes out in the language of the prophet Isaiah.

The kingdom condition, its role and ramifications on, through, and in society is an enduring question that all churches must explore. The people of God cannot ultimately be divorced from the culture in which they find themselves. The culture is not the same as the kingdom, nor can the kingdom and culture exist in separate walled-in spheres. This brings us back to attempting to answer those nagging questions. The people of God have to see what the ramifications of the kingdom, being in and among the people of God, mean for the local church. If the kingdom comes through the sharing of relationships, and the local church is the hermeneutic of the gospel to its community, then the local church must be engaged in society. This is why the positions of "Christ above culture" and "Christ the transformer of culture" are the most reasonable frameworks of approaching the kingdom and society.

10

The Role of Isaiah in the Life of Jesus

To discover the kingdom we need to discover Isaiah. Jesus quotes from Isaiah more than from any other book in the Bible. Moreover, the gospel writers attribute many of the passages in Isaiah to Jesus. One cannot have a true grasp on the motifs that appear in the Gospels without adequate readings in Isaiah. In this chapter we will explore a variety of motifs from the famous, like the suffering servant, to more subtle inclusions, such as the meek servant of the Lord. We also look at some of the interpretations of Jesus based on passages in Isaiah. Finally, we look at Isaiah for the work itself.

One must imagine that Jesus studied intensely this prophet who, in many ways, provided political, economic, and social context in first century Judaism. The work of Isaiah was relevant to Jesus the student, and served as a cornerstone for the teachings of Jesus. Isaiah, I believe, plays a huge role in the development of Christ's view of the last days, as well.

As you will see from examples that follow, it is clear that the authors of the Gospels, and Jesus himself relied heavily on Isaiah. Because of this, the book of Isaiah gives us great insight into the reality of Jesus and how he and the gospel writers saw his relationship with the kingdom.

DONKEY KNOWS HIS OWNER'S MANGER: ISAIAH 1:3

No two Christmas nativity displays are exactly alike. Dr. Brewer, the District Superintendent of Northern Missouri of the Assemblies of God, has well over two hundred nativities that he has collected

THE LAST DISCIPLE

during his tenure as a pastor and leader. Many are handcrafted; all are remarkable. Coming in various sizes, each is made with a uniqueness that is awe-inspiring. Some started in Africa as a block of wood, while others were molded in a factory. Regardless, each and every nativity features a donkey. Most people do not know that the presence of the donkey in the Christian nativity is inspired by the prophet Isaiah.

> *The ox knows his master, the donkey his owner's manger, but Israel does not know, my people do not understand.*
>
> ISAIAH 1:3 (NIV)

This verse at the beginning of Isaiah shows the book's serious implications for the reality of Christ's coming and for how we should read the gospels. If you read the birth narratives of Jesus closely you see that no donkey is reported in the story. However, what is reported is the manger. The Christian tradition associated this donkey with the manger; hence, popular retelling is with the donkey's inclusion. This manger and the associated donkey are narrative devices to help those reading the gospels see the prophetic connection between Jesus and Isaiah at the onset of his story. The donkey will later demonstrate the relationship Christ will have with his people, and will reveal the people's unfortunate response to his messianic reality. This becomes more evident as Jesus rides a donkey at the triumphal entry in all four gospels. According to Isaiah, the donkey will know his owner's manger, but Israel won't understand who their master will be.

IMMANUEL SIGNS: ISAIAH 7:14 AND 7:12

> *Therefore the Lord himself will give you a sign: The virgin will be with child and will give birth to a son, and will call him Immanuel.*
>
> ISAIAH 7:14 (NIV)

The Role of Isaiah in the Life of Jesus

Here we have perhaps the most-often quoted and used "proof text" for a fulfillment of Old Testament Scripture in the life of Christ. As we consider interpretations of this text, we should keep a few issues in mind. First, we must recognize that the original context is about the son of the Judean King Ahaz. King Ahaz ruled during a troublesome time, and Isaiah wanted King Ahaz to wait for God to give him support, instead of making alliances with Assyria. One only has to read the book of Isaiah to see that is clearly the case. In several chapters, Isaiah reiterates the problem of the entangling alliance. The second, and perhaps more difficult issue, revolves around the Hebrew word *almah*. *Almah* can be translated two ways. It can mean either "young woman" or it can mean "virgin." As we will see, Matthew's interpretation favors virgin. This problem of translation remains a point of contention between Jewish and Christian scholars. One would be wise to avoid the pitfall of quoting Isa 7:14 as a "Virgin Birth Proof Text."

> *But Ahaz said, I will not ask; I will not put the Lord to the test.*
> ISAIAH 7:12(NIV)

I find it ironic that Jesus uses the words of Ahaz in response to a test he faces in the book of Matthew.

> *Jesus answered him, "It is also written:*
> *'Do not put the Lord your God to the test.'"*
> MATTHEW 4:7 (NIV)

When Satan tests Jesus in the desert, Jesus testifies to Satan that he is exactly who Satan believes him to be. This literal quote of Isa 7:12 is a response to Satan who quotes the previous verse of Isaiah, which includes asking God for a sign on the deepest depth or highest heights. Think of that in the context of being high on the temple in the middle of the temptation. That's genius! After Satan quotes a portion of the passage, Jesus' response says, to the effect, "Yes, I am Immanuel . . . and I know the Isaiah scroll better than you!"

Given the interpretative reality of Matthew's Gospel (seeing Jesus as a typological fulfillment of Isa 7:14) and the other accounts of Jesus quoting from the same area, we can ascertain the messianic reality based in part on Isa 7:12. Moreover, seeing that the gospel writers have Jesus quoting from the book of Isaiah indicates that they see Jesus as the fulfillment of this prophecy. And if we believe their historic validity, it would seem as though Jesus understands himself to be born of a virgin and one who is the bringer of the kingdom. Still, let our case for Christ and kingdom not rest on these passages alone.

TO US A CHILD IS BORN, AND JUSTICE: ISAIAH 9

As we study Jesus through the lens of Isaiah, note that a full study linking Old Testament prophecy with Jesus is beyond the scope of this book. However, we can explore some essential connections. As I mention elsewhere in this book, the kingdom of God is Jesus' primary sermon topic, and yet we have trouble describing the kingdom as part of our ecclesiological reality. For this reason, it is vital we look to the book of Isaiah for guidance. When Jesus speaks about the kingdom of God, we must also think about the words of Isaiah because Jesus himself uses the work of Isaiah as a conceptual touchstone for this topic. With this in mind, let us look at Jesus himself, his conceptions of the kingdom of God, and how these are tied to the concept of justice in Isaiah. To do so, we must look at them through the lens of a key passage in Isaiah: the "to us a child is born" prophecy. (Keep in mind my prior thoughts in chapter 7 on the Old Testament covenantal assumption that fulfillment comes through children.) After we have studied this passage as demonstrative of the Messiah and justice, we will move to other passages related to justice.

The Role of Isaiah in the Life of Jesus

For to us a child is born, to us a son is given, and the government will be on his shoulders. And he will be called Wonderful Counselor, Mighty God, Everlasting Father, Prince of Peace. Of the increase of his government and peace there will be no end. He will reign on David's throne and over his kingdom, establishing and upholding it with justice and righteousness from that time on and forever.

ISAIAH 9:6–7 (NIV)

Now justice is mentioned thirty times in Isaiah. However, this theme is directly tied to prophecies about the Messiah. Let me list and comment on a few Messiah prophecies. This study allows us to see the commonality between justice, the kingdom, and the Messiah.

Zion will be redeemed with justice, her penitent ones with righteousness.

ISAIAH 1:27 (NIV)

But with righteousness he will judge the needy, with justice he will give decisions for the poor of the earth. He will strike the earth with the rod of his mouth; with the breath of his lips he will slay the wicked.

ISAIAH 11:4 (NIV)

See, a king will reign in righteousness and rulers will rule with justice.

ISAIAH 32:1 (NIV)

Here is my servant, whom I uphold, my chosen one in whom I delight; I will put my Spirit on him and he will bring justice to the nations.

ISAIAH 42:1 (NIV)

Notice, in this last verse, that these words, "my chosen one in whom I delight," are the same words used in the gospels as Jesus comes up out of the water at baptism. See Matthew 3:17 and Luke 3:21.

THE LAST DISCIPLE

> *A bruised reed he will not break, and a smoldering wick he will not snuff out. In faithfulness he will bring forth justice.*
>
> ISAIAH 42:3 (NIV)

If you read Matt 12:20, you'll notice this passage again. Here, Jesus recognizes his messianic uniqueness as he heals the sick and then warns his followers not to turn him into a political or populace leader. Jesus recognizes that he is not after the political allegiances offered by any earthly king. Jesus wants his followers to understand that their hearts and minds belong to God.

> *My righteousness draws near speedily, my salvation is on the way, and my arm will bring justice to the nations. The islands will look to me and wait in hope for my arm.*
>
> ISAIAH 51:5 (NIV)

By now, you may have discovered that, if you want to find the Messiah in Isaiah, look for the word justice. If you want to understand the underpinnings of Jesus' teaching of the kingdom, study how justice is described in Isaiah.

THE BRANCH OF JESSE: ISAIAH 11:1-12

> *A shoot will come up from the stump of Jesse; from his roots a Branch will bear fruit. The Spirit of the Lord will rest on him—the Spirit of wisdom and of understanding, the Spirit of counsel and of power, the Spirit of knowledge and of the fear of the Lord—and he will delight in the fear of the Lord. He will not judge by what he sees with his eyes, or decide by what he hears with his ears; but with righteousness he will judge the needy, with justice he will give decisions for the poor of the earth. He will strike the earth with the rod of his mouth; with the breath of his lips he will slay the wicked. Righteousness will be his belt and faithfulness the sash around his waist. The wolf will live with the lamb, the leopard will lie down with the goat, the calf and the lion and*

> the yearling together; and a little child will lead them. The cow will feed with the bear, their young will lie down together, and the lion will eat straw like the ox. The infant will play near the hole of the cobra, and the young child put his hand into the viper's nest. They will neither harm nor destroy on all my holy mountain, for the earth will be full of the knowledge of the Lord as the waters cover the sea. In that day the Root of Jesse will stand as a banner for the peoples; the nations will rally to him, and his place of rest will be glorious. In that day the Lord will reach out his hand a second time to reclaim the remnant that is left of his people from Assyria, from Lower Egypt, from Upper Egypt, from Cush, from Elam, from Babylonia, from Hamath and from the islands of the sea. He will raise a banner for the nations and gather the exiles of Israel; he will assemble the scattered people of Judah from the four quarters of the earth.
>
> ISAIAH 11:1–12 (NIV)

Isaiah strongly develops the messianic theme and the reality of the Messiah's reign, which includes a time of peace and restructure. Notice that Isaiah outlines exactly from where this individual Messiah will come. This Messiah will be a shoot that develops out of the stump of David. One does not need to look very far to discover that the Hebrew term for *branch (netser)* is related to the name of the town Nazareth (in Hebrew, *natseret*). Of course, we know this was where Jesus experienced his childhood, and it explains why we have a specific reference in Matthew.[1]

> And he went and lived in a town called Nazareth.
> So was fulfilled what was said through the prophets,
> that he would be called a Nazarene.
>
> MATTHEW 2:23 (NIV)

The result of the reign of the Messiah is true peace. Peace is absorbed in every aspect of the social strata. The image of this

1. Beyer, Encountering the Book of Isaiah, 89.

peace includes mortal enemies in the animal kingdom becoming playmates. It is as though the natural state of the kingdom brings all living things back into Eden-like harmony. It is difficult to determine if Isaiah is pointing us back to Eden, or if he is pointing us toward the eschatological reality that takes place with the coming of the Messiah. The important concept is that the Messiah reassembles the Diaspora of his people. This uniting of Israel fits with the concept that the Messiah has the likeness of David. The kingdom, which is established on the justice of its King, comes together because it is established by a just measure; and the people do not fear their neighbor's injustice or their own, because of the greatness of their King's reign.

THE MEEK SERVANT OF THE LORD: ISAIAH 42

Here is my servant, whom I uphold, my chosen one in whom I delight; I will put my Spirit on him and he will bring justice to the nations. He will not shout or cry out, or raise his voice in the streets. A bruised reed he will not break, and a smoldering wick he will not snuff out. In faithfulness he will bring forth justice; he will not falter or be discouraged till he establishes justice on earth. In his law the islands will put their hope.

ISAIAH 42:1–4 (NIV)

The aspect of the kingdom-bringer, as already discussed, is perhaps the most conspicuous aspect of justice. However, let's focus on the servant's actions. In this passage, notice the distinction between the way justice is brought forth and the manner in which the Ruler carries it out in his reign. Peace becomes reality by way of what appears to be unorthodox means. There are no revolutionary actions or even wartime cries. It is as though this justice comes in the middle of the night without the unsavory results that often accompany a new rule of governance or leadership. No hostile takeover here. I cannot help but think of the late, great Dr. Martin Luther King Jr.'s principals for sit-ins. Dr. King learned about non-violence from

The Role of Isaiah in the Life of Jesus

Jesus, and I think of several verses where Jesus suggested principles of non-violence, such as turning the other cheek. (See Matt 5:5, 23-24, 38-39, 40-41, and 43-44. Also see Luke 9:51-56. I will quote from only Matt 5:5 and 5:38-39 here.)

> *Blessed are the meek, for they will inherit the earth.*
>
> MATTHEW 5:5 (NIV)

> *You have heard it said, "Eye for eye, tooth for tooth." But I tell you, do not resist an evil person. If anyone slaps you on the right cheek, turn to them the other cheek also.*
>
> MATTHEW 5:38-39 (NIV)

Note that there are no street demonstrations to demand justice. Yet, we see incredible determination by the servant to endure and not to falter.

THE REIGN OF GOD: ISAIAH 52

Isaiah 52 is perhaps the best biblical description of how the "kingdom comes." In particular: "You were sold for nothing, and without money you will be redeemed" (Isa 52:3). Isaiah is saying that, at some point, God is going to restore the nation of Israel. As the Israelites were forced into physical captivity without compensation, so they will be free without bribe or payment. Imagine the typology of those who are in spiritual bonds. They will be freed through the future work of Jesus on the cross. This theme echoes throughout Jesus' life and through his disciples to the point that it is picked up by Peter and is articulated in 1 Peter.

> *For you know that it was not with perishable things such as silver or gold that you were redeemed from the empty way of life handed down to you from you forefathers.*
>
> 1 PETER 1:18 (NIV)

THE LAST DISCIPLE

THE REJECTED SERVANT OF THE LORD: ISAIAH 53

Who has believed our message and to whom has the arm of the Lord been revealed? He grew up before him like a tender shoot, and like a root out of dry ground. He had no beauty or majesty to attract us to him, nothing in his appearance that we should desire him. He was despised and rejected by men, a man of sorrows, and familiar with suffering. Like one from whom men hide their faces he was despised, and we esteemed him not. Surely he took up our infirmities and carried our sorrows, yet we considered him stricken by God, smitten by him, and afflicted. But he was pierced for our transgressions, he was crushed for our iniquities; the punishment that brought us peace was upon him, and by his wounds we are healed. We all, like sheep, have gone astray, each of us has turned to his own way; and the Lord has laid on him the iniquity of us all. He was oppressed and afflicted, yet he did not open his mouth; he was led like a lamb to the slaughter, and as a sheep before her shearers is silent, so he did not open his mouth. By oppression and judgment he was taken away. And who can speak of his descendants? For he was cut off from the land of the living; for the transgression of my people he was stricken. He was assigned a grave with the wicked, and with the rich in his death, though he had done no violence, nor was any deceit in his mouth. Yet it was the Lord's will to crush him and cause him to suffer, and though the Lord makes his life a guilt offering, he will see his offspring and prolong his days, and the will of the Lord will prosper in his hand. After the suffering of his soul, he will see the light of life and be satisfied; by his knowledge my righteous servant will justify many, and he will bear their iniquities.

Isaiah 53:1–11 (NIV)

When I consider the beginning of Isa 53, I often think of the motif of messianic secrecy in the book of Mark. In Mark, we find Jesus constantly telling those he has healed not to tell anyone what had happened.

The Role of Isaiah in the Life of Jesus

And Jesus healed many who had various diseases. He also drove out many demons, but he would not let the demons speak because they knew who he was.

MARK 1:34 (NIV)

"But what about you?" he asked. "Who do you say I am?" Peter answered, "You are the Messiah." Jesus warned them not to tell anyone about him.

MARK 8:29-30 (NIV)

These are but a few of the many Markan passages in which Jesus conceals himself. This secrecy is consistent with Isa 52, which includes the servant shutting the mouths of the rulers of the earth. But let us not forget that Isa 53 begins: "Who has believed our message," and "To whom has the arm of the Lord been revealed?" That is, Isaiah reminds us to anticipate the nature of the kingdom of God and its reign. This would seem to be a reversal of thought. However, if you look back to Isa 42, you will see that this secrecy and anticipation fits hand in glove. Look at these verses: Isa 42:2 and 23.

He will not shout or cry out or raise his voice in the streets.

ISAIAH 42:2 (NIV)

Which of you will listen to this or pay close attention in time to come?

ISAIAH 42:23 (NIV)

The theme of Isa 53 and the passages related in the gospels demonstrate the surprising and secretive nature of the kingdom. Isaiah's depiction of the rejected servant demonstrates that this messianic secrecy is part of God's will. The gospel writers also continue in this tradition by showing Jesus as one who, at times, concealed his true identity. It is not the popularity of the kingdom or the Messiah that rejuvenates humanity. To the contrary, humanity is rejuvenated by the ability of the Messiah to suffer in substitutionary satisfaction. However, Isaiah goes even further. In Isaiah, those who see the suffering servant look at him like Job's friends looked at Job. They believe that the servant has done something to deserve punishment from God. Thus, it is doubly shameful on those who "esteem him not." Not only does the servant receive injustice for acting justly, but he is shunned by humanity because we believe him to be unjust and punished by God for being so. The implication is that the Messiah does this because the expectations of the kingdom aren't congruent with the values of the world. If we see Jesus as the Messiah, then this fits with the way he brings the kingdom. The kingdom begins with a Messiah who dies between two thieves in the place of the Skull.

JESUS' KINGDOM, ISAIAH'S KINGDOM

The gospel writers saw Jesus as the Messiah figure depicted in Isaiah. This is demonstrated by their use of text from a large body of Isaiah scriptures. Jesus saw himself as the Messiah figure in the book of Isaiah. This belief is demonstrated in Jesus' many quotations from Isaiah that he associates to himself. One especially telling quotation is in Isa 7:12. Here Jesus quotes from Isaiah's "Immanuel" passage to overcome Satan and to show Satan his belief in his own deity. If the gospel writers and Jesus himself associate Jesus with the Messiah figure in Isaiah, then we have to look at how Isaiah depicts the Messiah's kingdom to understand Jesus' view of the kingdom of God. How does Isaiah see the kingdom? Isaiah's major theme of the kingdom is justice. This justice is marked by peace, righteousness, and the destruction of evil. (See Isa 1:27, 11:4, and 32:1). It's also a kingdom ruled by a gentle ruler (Isa 42:3). It's not a political kingdom but one that restructures the very foundations of the earth to the very natural state of all living creatures (Isa 11:1–42). The Messiah will gather his people from the four corners of the earth (Isa 11:10-12). How does the kingdom come? The kingdom of justice comes by a servant who is meek. It comes not in a violent revolutionary overthrow but by the peaceful endurance of the faithful servant (Isa 42). Finally the kingdom comes in surprising and secretive ways. This is Isaiah's understanding of the Messiah and the kingdom. When Jesus enters his public ministry declaring the nearness of the kingdom of God, he is proclaiming what the condition of the people of God should be and will be. This condition (Isaiah's kingdom description) is the culture that the local church should exemplify.

11

Jesus' Eschatology and the Call to Faithfulness

JESUS' ESCHATOLOGY is a call to faithfulness and unity. If you think that Jesus is a prophet who will brings in the last days without concern for the everyday underlying structure of our society, then you would be sorely mistaken. Jesus clearly describes both the needs of our current society and of the one to come. The following verses demonstrate this dual concern.

> *Looking at his disciples, he said: "Blessed are you who are poor, for yours is the kingdom of God."*
>
> LUKE 6:20 (NIV)

> *Blessed are the poor in spirit, for theirs is the kingdom of heaven.*
>
> MATTHEW 5:3 (NIV)

The passage in Luke emphasizes "blessed are the poor." Matthew emphasizes the "poor in spirit." While Matthew's gospel localizes the blessing spiritually, Luke's gospel localizes the blessing on being poor. These examples are demonstrative of each gospel's specific emphasis on the future kingdom.

As these passages illustrate, Jesus is concerned about the poverty of spirit in our current society and concerned about the eschatological implications its future. Perhaps it is a cue for us when Jesus says, "No person knows the hour except the Father." [1] The implication is that Jesus himself does not even know, or cares

---

1. Matt 24:36 (NIV).

Jesus' Eschatology and the Call to Faithfulness

to know, about the time of his own return. Rather his concern for his disciples is that they go into their societies and minister. For the first century disciples it was Jerusalem, Judea, Samaria and beyond. Our focus on the eschaton to the exclusion of today's real-world needs is not consistent with the words of Jesus himself.

Jesus' prophetic address from Matt 24 and 25 is an important passage in this regard. A few comments are worth considering before studying these chapters. Sometimes section titles are not helpful in our Bibles. Many have divorced Matt 24 and 25 from the needs of society, and in so doing have interpreted these passages without looking at what they mean for our present condition. While these signs indeed indicate the end of the age, they also illustrate a neglectful society. In Matt 24 and 25, Jesus answers the disciples' questions: What will be the sign of your coming, and the end of the age?[2] Jesus says to the disciples that when they give a cup of cold water in his name, they are doing this unto him. If they go visit people in prison they are doing this in his name.[3] In a very real sense, Jesus is talking about the very present day in which they live. This is the current situation in which they find themselves.

This previous passage is about the end of the age. But let's remember that the point of the larger passage is *what are you doing now?* Regardless, we also search for eschatological interpretations in Scripture, and so we look at this passage in the context of the book of Revelation. So let us think about this passage in the context of Revelation too.

Revelation is a difficult book. It is so difficult that it took decades of canonization for us to accept it into our Scriptures. Nonetheless, as you read Revelation, you will discover that, in the end, Jesus is victor. But perhaps the primary reason why Revelation was written and canonized is because it is also a call to be faithful. This theme echoes throughout the book. (See Rev 1:5; 2:10, 13; 3:10, 14; 14:12; 17:14; and 19:11.) I believe this call to faith

2. Matt 24:3 (NIV).
3. Matt 25:36 (NIV).

is missing in our eschatological component as we think and talk about the future coming and reigning of the kingdom. We must be faithful. God calls us to faithfulness. He calls us to continue to follow as disciples in these endeavors, such as being with the poor, feeding the hungry, and going to those held captive. The problems have always been in our world. These problems will always be in our world until a faithful people see those problems to conclusion. But let's delve deeper into the subject of Jesus and eschatology—we have two eschatological schools in conflict. This conflict is centered mostly on conflicting interpretations of Matt 24–25. If you plan on stopping to read these chapters, I would suggest that you do so now. This is a long passage and I suggest you read it all at once to get a full context.

One school of interpretation champions an approach that says, in effect, that we must provide Jesus the keys of the kingdom in order for the end time to begin. That is, if we can just work out our problems, he will come; if we can just get the problems in our societies solved, it will usher in his kingdom. One of the strengths of this view is that it promotes a spirit of optimism rather than pessimism. Still, it can be overly unrealistic.

The other school champions an approach that emphasizes the cataclysmic reality of the apocalypse. Implicit in this view is the tendency to resort to an attitude of earthly abandonment. If it's all going to be destroyed, what's the value in improvement? Society is going to continually spiral downward until this apocalyptic destruction finishes it off. Still, this view takes very seriously the dramatic nature of what Jesus describes as signs of the end.

Both schools offer valuable interpretations of Matt 24-25; though I would argue that extreme interpretations do little to address the actual theological burdens we carry.

Those who ascribe to the first approach are susceptible to the slow fade of distinguishing kingdom values versus cultural values. And this is one of the dangers to not heeding Jesus' words of immediacy. Those who ascribe to the second approach's interpretation often create entrenched, close-knit Christian communities. "Well, after all, what are we going to do? The world's just going to continue to get worse, and there's nothing we can do about it. The true problem with this extreme eschatology, however, is that it provides little evangelistic need for the compassion of one's neighbor.

Those who ascribe to the approach of the first view tend to emphasize social improvement above all other concerns. On the surface this approach would seem to meet the real-world challenges that Jesus tasks his disciples to meet. However, adherents of this approach tend to focus more on communal and political influence on society, and can neglect the moral and individual responsibility of personal evangelism.

Let's strike a tension here and talk about how Jesus connects both implications of these interpretations. Although Jesus would never couch them in these two eschatological schools of thought, I believe he would say that we are individually responsible, but at the same time there are spiritual influencers beyond our individual and ecclesiastical control. At the end of the day, I believe, Jesus would remind us that the sovereignty of God is our ultimate influence. Jesus' eschatology always calls us to be faithful in our practice of living. This is true in his communication in the gospels and is a primary theme of Revelation. Jesus calls not simply for us to be faithful individually, but also socially, no matter how bad a society may get.

It is amazing how many Christians have believed they were experiencing the last days. Some members of the first church during the time of Nero and the fall of the Roman Empire thought they would experience the return of Christ, and their influence was global because they remained faithful. Individuals in many African nations today believe they are in the tribulation because of their great suffering. And yet, their influence is great, because they are faithful. Let us follow and answer that call.

By this I mean we have got to come to a place where we will serve. Service, in this context, is related to a greater conversation about personal evangelism and social compassion. You have to do both, and you have to both *well*. You have to care. You have to really mean it when you say that you care about other people, that you love them. This compassion must be the manifestation of Jesus' love. Church programs and church cultures that are based on the love of Jesus can be effective. If we fail in our responsibility to our neighbor and society, we have missed the call of Jesus Christ. The deeper your relationship with Jesus, the more your eschatology will be lived out now. This is the true expression of the nearness of the kingdom in Jesus' eschatology, and why he says repent for the kingdom of God is near.[4]

THE KINGDOM COMPONENT OF ESCHATOLOGY

In regard to the return of Christ and the Kingdom, we need to be careful that we don't make the same mistakes that some made during the time of Christ. Many of these people wondered when Christ would set up his political and earthly reign. But Jesus was very careful to side-step their enticing desire. Moreover, this was offered in a number of places and by a number of people, including Satan. Throughout his life and ministry, Jesus made it very clear that he was interested in the allegiance of men's hearts being for his Father. I wonder if we self-impose our own thinking about what will happen at the return of Christ. Much thinking, I fear, is in the line of triumphalism, perhaps even as some of the disciples were mistaken about the nature of the future. We also could be in danger ourselves.

Jesus had a united-kingdom eschatology. In what has been called his high priestly prayer, Jesus prays that his disciples may be one, as he and the Father are one. The real focus of John 17 is an eventual church that is not a divided but a united one.

---

4. Luke 10:9 (NIV).

Jesus' Eschatology and the Call to Faithfulness

My prayer is not for them alone. I pray also for those who will believe in me through their message, that all of them may be one, Father, just as you are in me and I am in you. May they also be in us so that the world may believe that you have sent me. I have given them the glory that you gave me, that they may be one as we are one—I in them and you in me—so that they may be brought to complete unity. Then the world will know that you sent me and have loved them even as you have loved me.

JOHN 17:20–23 (NIV)

It is significant that Jesus prayed this as his earthly mission was coming to a close. The theological richness should not be missed. In his prayer, Jesus reiterates his relationship to his Father. This should remind us that the model for the community comes from the authentic unity in the Trinity. As the Triune God is one, so we are to be as well. According to Ephesians, this will be a mark of our maturity. In Eph 4, Paul writes about equipping a five-fold ministry for the building up of the body: ". . . until we all reach unity in the faith and in the knowledge of the Son of God and become mature."[5] This passage in Ephesians has many references to Christ's work.

A good working eschatology emphasizes that Christ is coming for a church united and faithful in praise, in life, and with people ready to be united with all things in heaven and on earth in the supremacy of Christ. Let us be found faithful.

His master replied, "Well done, good and faithful servant! You have been faithful with a few things; I will put you in charge of many things. Come and share your master's happiness!"

MATTHEW 25:21 (NIV)

---

5. Eph 4:12–13 (NIV).

12

Conclusion

WE HAVE looked at the identity of the church, the theology that is behind it, the challenges it faces (including postmodernity), and some practices that can help reengage the church in the ministry of discipleship. Importance is often in the details. It is clear that the Pentecostal's ecclesiology is missional. This missional element must be intelligible to a local church's community in order for it to be a gospel that that community can understand. The missional elements come through in the practical realities of the church, but these realities become "theologized," because they create narratives that the local community sees as gospel.

The Bible gives Christians their theology, but the beginnings of the theology of a local community are its Christians. Continuous culture-change plays a role in the constant reinvention of church ministry; this includes the use of technology and reaching new people groups. Let us not syncretize to the culture of consumerism, but let us contextualize the gospel for the postmodern. Let our mission call us to become the deep thinkers of the future church. Let us embrace our church challenges with a radical self-abandon, like Jesus did.

We can use our position to positively influence our communities. But we must also pray. We must pray that people will have a life of determination to follow Christ. I am deeply convinced that we are missing a deep and wide prayer movement that engages the Spirit to help strengthen our weaknesses. Discipleship is not something that God gives to us or does for us. We must do it ourselves. We must be determined to follow Christ. The Spirit can help us achieve that personal will in a way that words cannot express, but we must be determined to live as Christ. Our redemption through the practice of continual repentance is part of that determination. When we do this through humility, we begin to develop character. Humility is the method by which all of the other aspects of our character can be developed. The determination to follow Christ's mission comes through the experience of seeing why Christ's mission should be our own.

The heart of God is embodied in us when we love him more than life itself, and when we love others more than ourselves. This happens only through deeply focused spiritual life. We must pay attention to the darker portions of our soul and see that the light within this darkness is really God illuminating our humanity. When we come to the end of ourselves, we begin in him. When we die, our hearts beat anew with the same blood that ran down the cross and that still flows through his veins. Let us embody the character, mission, and heart of Jesus Christ. Jesus, through his life, altered the course of human history. When we embody who he is, we alter history through changing another life, yet once again.

What we do in these moments matter as much for that next disciple as it did when Jesus came to Peter, James, and John. And they weren't his last disciples, nor will you be. But there will be one last disciple. You must see this truth if you take the scriptures seriously. This is the immediacy of the kingdom of God. And there will be one last disciple for your town, for your church, and for your family. What would it change if you knew who they were?

This is your invitation to begin discipleship again. Do so in the context of a faith community that embraces the understanding that the kingdom of God cannot be divorced from the culture in which it finds itself, nor can it associate this culture as being the same as the kingdom. Understand how engaging culture requires that you think about the local church as your community's lens of interpretation for the gospel. Engage the challenges that we face as a church by putting yourself in a position to practice well. Let Jesus' model of incarnation be our guide.

Glossary of Terms

anthropomorphism. Using human characteristics (it's all we have) in an attempt to describe God, an infinite being beyond human articulation. "God is love." "God is our source." "God is above all and in all." (This is a specific use of the term in theology.)

Christology. The study of theology related to Jesus Christ, including human and divine scopes.

Christocentric. Christ in the center of a certain theological or philosophical doctrine or personal belief.

codices (codex). An old manuscript with a binding and, usually, a cover. For example, Codex Sinaiticus is a manuscript from the 1600s, which contains the Christian Bible written in Greek.

ecclesiology. The study of the local church and *the* church. Attempts to answer: What do you need to constitute a church? What is the relationship of a local church and the kingdom?

epistemology. The study of the nature of knowledge and its limits. This branch of philosophy attempts to answer questions like: What can I know? What am I responsible for knowing? I consider it the bridge between philosophy's quest for truth and theological faith. Important field for postmodernists.

etiology. The study of origins. How things began and why they are now in their present state.

eschatology. The study of future events with Christ's return as the culmination of the end of current state.

Glossary of Terms

evangelical. Defined best by David Bebbington's quadrilateral. (1) Evangelicals are conversionists. They believe in the new birth, being saved. (2) Evangelicals take biblical authority, the supreme authority of the Scriptures with the utmost seriousness. (3) Evangelicals promote an activism. They believe that every Christian has to be involved in the work of the kingdom through evangelism, promoting social justice, working for peace, dealing with the moral health of the society. (4) Evangelical theology is cross-centered with Christ's atoning as the centerpiece of our thinking.

Free Church. Refers to churches that operate independently from other churches and denomination bodies. They are autonomous. Although free churches may share fellowship with other local churches there is no formal governance among organizations.

gnosticism. A higher knowledge or wisdom that is out of the reaches of many, usually expressed with dualism and separation of physical and spiritual. Tends to lead to other errors of how one views their body and their spirit.

imago Dei. Latin for image of God. The theological belief that humanity is created in the image of God and therefore has infinite value regardless of utility or functionality.

Kantian categorical (imperative). Individuals should act in only such a way that what they do should be universal for everyone else.

materialism. A philosophical bend in some societies that hold, along with other beliefs, that physical things have great importance.

metanarrative. An explanation of a big story, similar to a worldview based on personal experiences.

minuscules. A manuscript (New Testament's are Greek) that is in all lower case letters and squeezed together tightly.

Glossary of Terms

Missio Dei. Latin for the Action or Mission of God. Mission is not simply an activity of the church but a recognition that we do it because God is a missionary God.

Nicene Creed. Also called the Niceno—Constantinopolitan Creed. Most used Christian creed, which is a profession of faith and includes theology of the incarnation, double precession of the Holy Spirit, and the Trinity.

ontology. The study of existence or reality.

soteriology. The study of the theology of salvation.

Perichoresis. The mutual inter-penetration and indwelling within the threefold nature of the Trinity: God the Father, Jesus the Son, and the Holy Spirit. Originates with the church Father Gregory of Nazianzus.

postmodernism. A philosophy after modernity that is generally skeptical of syllogistic or linear logic. Also rejects modernity's notion of foundational assumptions of philosophy, theology, and scientific bodies of thought. Considered by some to be indefensible; it argues that the philosopher cannot distinguish between ignorance and knowledge.

postmillennialism. Eschatological and consequentially social theory about Christ's return after a "Golden Age of Christianity."

premillennialism. Eschatological and consequentially social theory about Christ's return before his physical and spiritual rule on the earth.

theodicy. Branch of theology that attempts to reconcile the belief of a good God with the problem of evil.

secularization. The transformation of society toward non-religious values.

Second Temple Judaism. The practice of Judaism between 516 BC and 70 AD. The type of Judaism practiced during

Glossary of Terms

Christ's time on the earth and at which time much of the New Testament is written.

Uncials. A manuscript (New Testament's are Greek) that is in all capital letters.

Bibliography

Anderson, A. H., and W. J. Hollenweger, eds., *Pentecostals after a Century: Global Perspectives on a Movement in Transition.* London: Sheffield Academic, 1999.

Anderson, Leith. *Church for the 21st Century.* Minneapolis, MN: Bethany House, 1992.

Aquinas, Thomas. *Summa Theologica*, (portions). English edition is that of the Fathers of the English Dominican Province, *The Summa Theologica of St. Thomas Aquinas.* London: Burns, Oates & Washbourne, 1912–1925.

Bettenson, Henry, and Chris Maunder. *Documents of the Christian Church.* New York: Oxford University Press, 1999.

Beyer, B. E. *Encountering the Book of Isaiah.* Grand Rapids, MI: Baker Academic, 2007.

Buechner, Fredrick. *Telling Secrets.* New York: HarperOne, 1992.

Burgess, Stanley. *New International Dictionary of Pentecostal and Charismatic Movements.* Grand Rapids, MI: Zondervan, 2002.

Carson, D. A., ed. *Telling the Truth: Evangelizing Postmodernists.* Grand Rapids, MI: Zondervan, 2000.

Deacy, Christopher. *Screen Christologies: Redemption and the Medium of Film.* Cardiff, Wales: University of Wales Press, 2001.

Drislane, Robert and Gary Parkinson. *Online Dictionary of the Social Sciences.* Online: http://bitbucket.icaap.org/dict.pl.

Epp, Eldon J., and Gordon Fee. *Studies in the Theory and Method of New Testament Textual Criticism.* Downers Grove, IL: InterVarsity, 1993.

Fee, Gordon. *The First Epistle to the Corinthians.* New International Commentary on the New Testament (NICNT), Grand Rapids, MI: Eerdmans, 1987.

Fiddes, Paul. *Participating in God: A Pastoral Doctrine of the Trinity.* Louisville, KY: Westminster John Knox, 2001.

Freidberg, Anne. "Cinema and the Postmodern Condition" in *Viewing Positions: Ways of Seeing Film.* Edited by Linda Williams. Piscataway, NJ: Rutgers University Press, 1995.

Freud, Sigmund. *Civilization and Its Discontents.* New York: Norton, 1930.

Gibbs, Eddie. "Evangelizing Nominal Christians." Pasadena, CA: Lecture, Fuller Theological Seminary, summer 2005.

Bibliography

———. *In Name Only: Evangelizing Nominal Christians*. Wheaton, IL: BridgePoint/Victor Books, 1994.

Green, Joel, and Stuart Palmer, eds. *In Search of the Soul: Four Views of the Mind-Body Problem*. Downers Grove: InterVarsity, 2005.

Grenz, Stanley J. *Theology for the Community of God*. Grand Rapids, MI: Eerdmans, 2000.

Grenz, Stanley, et al. *Pocket Dictionary of Theological Terms*. Downers Grove, IL: InterVarsity, 1999.

Gross, Paul R., and Norman Levitt. *Higher Superstition: The Academic Left and its Quarrel with Science*. Baltimore: John Hopkins, 1993.

Hillerbrand, Hans J., ed. *The Protestant Reformation*. New York: Harper & Row, 1968.

Hollenweger, Walter J. "From Azusa Street to the Toronto Phenomenon: Historical Roots of the Pentecostal Movement," *Concilium* 3 (1996), 3–14.

Hunsberger, George R. *Bearing the Witness of the Spirit: Lesslie Newbigin's Theology of Cultural Plurality*. Grand Rapids, MI: Eerdmans, 1998.

Kallenberg, Brad. *Live to Tell; Evangelism for a Postmodern Age*. Grand Rapids, MI: Brazos, 2002.

Kärkkäinen, Veli-Matti. *An Introduction to Ecclesiology*. Downers Grove, IL: InterVarsity, 2002.

———. "Systematic Theology III, Ecclesiology and Eschatology." Lecture, Fuller Theological Seminary, Pasadena, CA, March 2006.

———. *Toward a Pneumatological Theology*. Lanham, MD: University Press of America, 2002.Kenny, Anthony, ed. *The Wittgenstein Reader*. Hoboken, NJ: Wiley Blackwell, 1994.

Ladd, George. *The Presence of the Future*. Grand Rapids, MI: Eerdmans, 2002.

Latourette, Kenneth S. *A History of Christianity, Volume I: Beginnings to 1500*. San Francisco: HarperCollins, 1975.

McLaren, Brian. *Church on the Other Side*. Grand Rapids, MI: Zondervan, 2003.

Metzger, Bruce. *A Textual Commentary on the Greek New Testament*. New York: UBS, 1994.

Miller, Perry. *The Errand in the Wilderness*. Cambridge: Harvard University Press, 1956.

Miller, Walter. *A Canticle for Leibowitz*. Bantam Spectra, 1959.

Motyer, J. Alec. *Isaiah: An Introduction and Commentary*. Tyndale Old Testament Commentaries (TOTC), Downers Grove, IL: InterVarsity, 1999.

Murphy, Nancey. *Anglo-American Postmodernity: Philosophical Perspectives on Science, Religion, and Ethics*. Boulder, CO: Westview, 1997.

Bibliography

Neuhaus, Richard John. *Catholic Matters, Confusion, Controversy, and the Splendor of Truth.* Jackson, TN: Basic Books, 2007.

Newbigin, Leslie. *Truth to Tell: The Gospel as Public Truth.* Grand Rapids, MI: Eerdmans, 1991.

Niebuhr, H. Richard. *Christ and Culture.* New York: Harper, 1951.

Noll, Mark. *A History of Christianity in the United States and Canada.* Grand Rapids, MI: Eerdmans, 1992.

Ott, Ludwig. *Fundamentals of Catholic Dogma.* Charlotte, NC: Tan Books, 1974.

Pannenberg, Wolfhart. *Theology and the Kingdom of God.* Louisville, KY: Westminster, 1969.

Pinnock, Clark H. *Flame of Love: A Theology of the Holy Spirit.* Downers Grove, IL: InterVarsity, 1996.

Plato. *The Republic.* Translated by Benjamin Jowett. New York: The Modern Library, Book VII, 1941.

Pope-Levison, Priscilla, and John R. Levision. *Jesus in Global Contexts.* Louisville, KY: John Knox, 1992.

Sanders, N. K. *The Epic of Gilgamesh.* (Translation 1960), London: Penguin, 1972.

Shields, Steven. "Delight and Dangers of Navigating Postmodern Currents, Part 2." Online: http://www.next-wave.org/mar01/shields2.htm.

Shuster, Marguerite. *The Fall and Sin, What We Have Become as Sinners.* Grand Rapids, MI: Eerdmans, 2004.

Sider, Ron. *Rich Christians in an Age of Hunger.* Nashville, TN: Thomas Nelson, 2005.

Sollier, Joseph. "Apollinarianism." *The Catholic Encyclopedia*, Vol. 1. New York: Robert Appleton, 1907.

Stassen, Glen, and David Gushee. *Kingdom Ethics, Following Jesus in Contemporary Context.* Downers Grove, IL: InterVarsity, 2003.

Tozer, A. W. *The Pursuit of God.* Camp Hill, PA: Christian Publications, 1982.

VanGelder, Craig. *The Essence of the Church.* Grand Rapids, MI: Baker, 2000.

Wagner, Peter C. *The Healthy Church.* Ventura, CA: Regal, 1996.

Wright, N. T. *Surprised by Hope.* New York: HarperOne, 2008.

Zacharias, Ravi. *The End of Reason.* Grand Rapids, MI:Zondervan, 2008.

www.ingramcontent.com/pod-product-compliance
Lightning Source LLC
Chambersburg PA
CBHW062002180426
43198CB00036B/2138